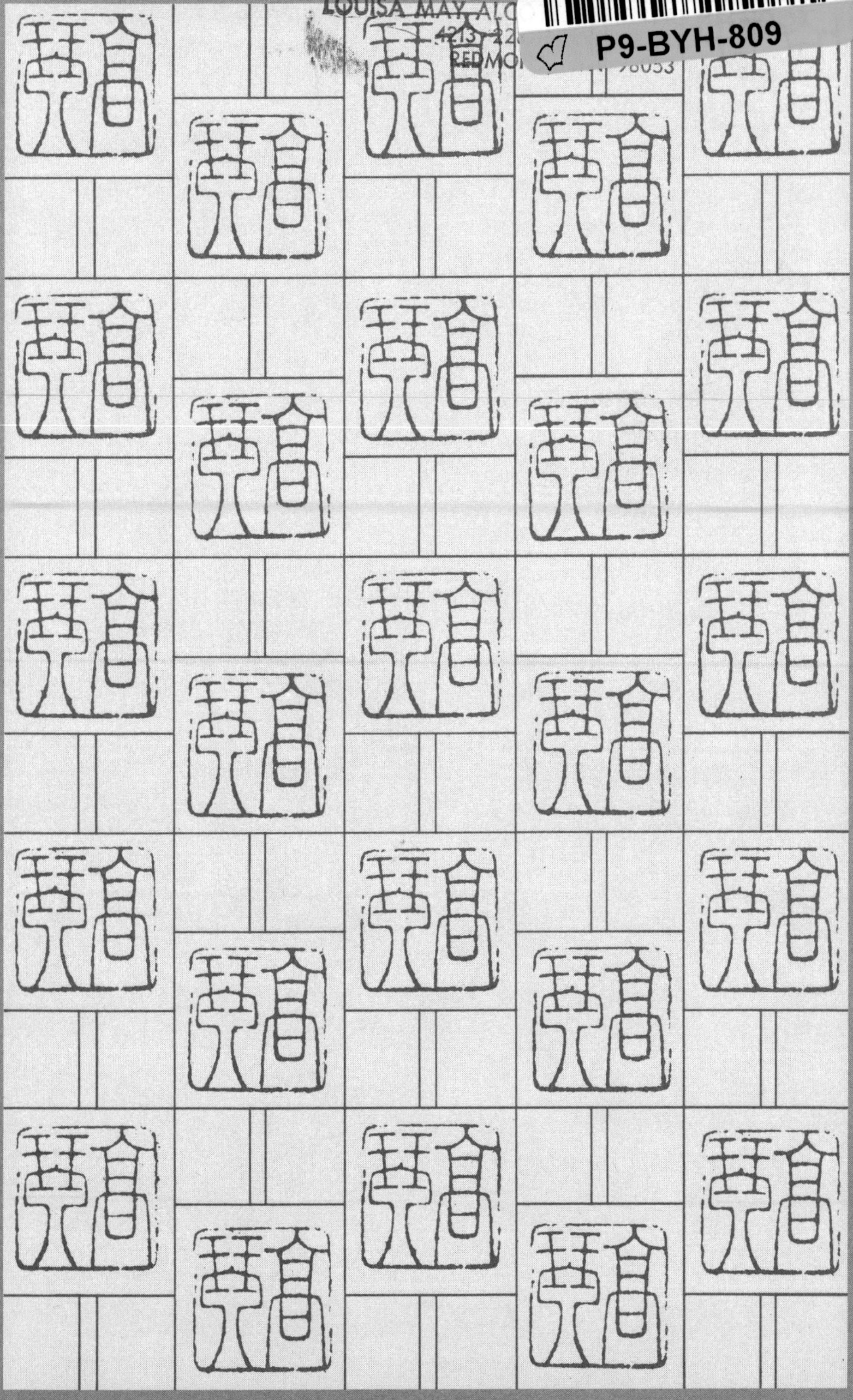

CHINA HOMECOMING

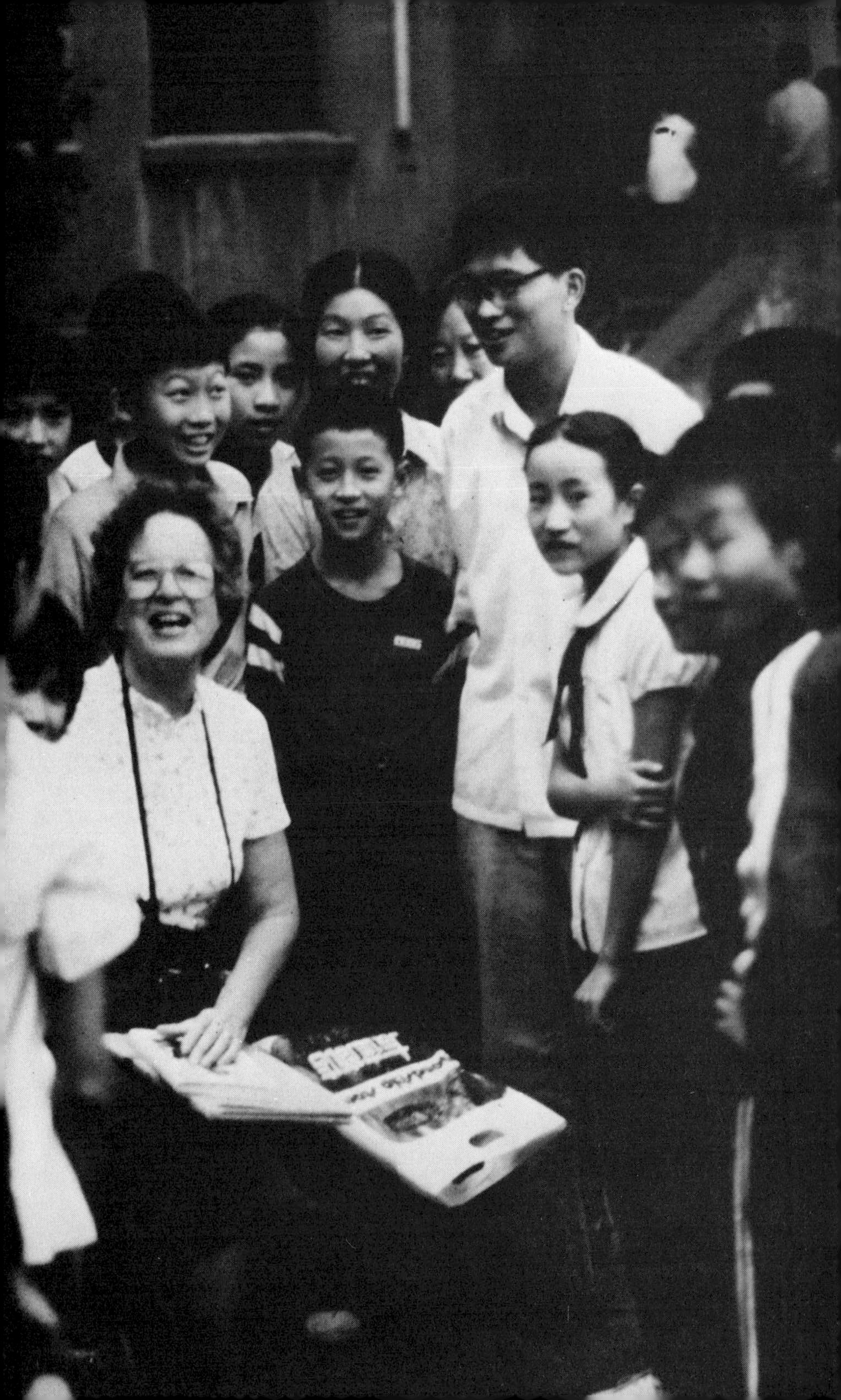

China Homecoming

JEAN FRITZ

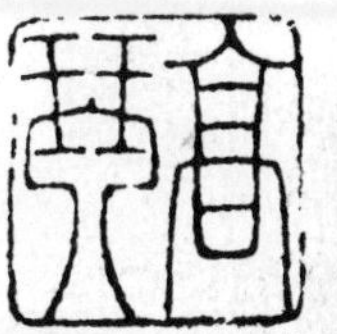

WITH PHOTOGRAPHS BY
MICHAEL FRITZ

G. P. PUTNAM'S SONS
New York

 Published simultaneously in
Canada by General Publishing Co. Limited, Toronto.
Printed in the United States of America

First Impression

Book design by Kathleen Westray

Library of Congress Cataloging in Publication Data
Fritz, Jean. China homecoming.
Bibliography: p.
1. China—Description and travel—1976-
2. Fritz, Jean. I. Title.
DS712.F74 1985 951′.212 [B] 84-24775
ISBN 0-399-21182-9

TO ANDREA DAY
WHO SHOULD HAVE BEEN ALONG

And with thanks to all those who helped me go:
Frances Roots Hadden, Chih-ping Sobelman,
Kuo Ho and Irene Chang, Martin Wilbur, John Starr,
Michael Gasster, Cynthia Chan, and Hedy Plew.

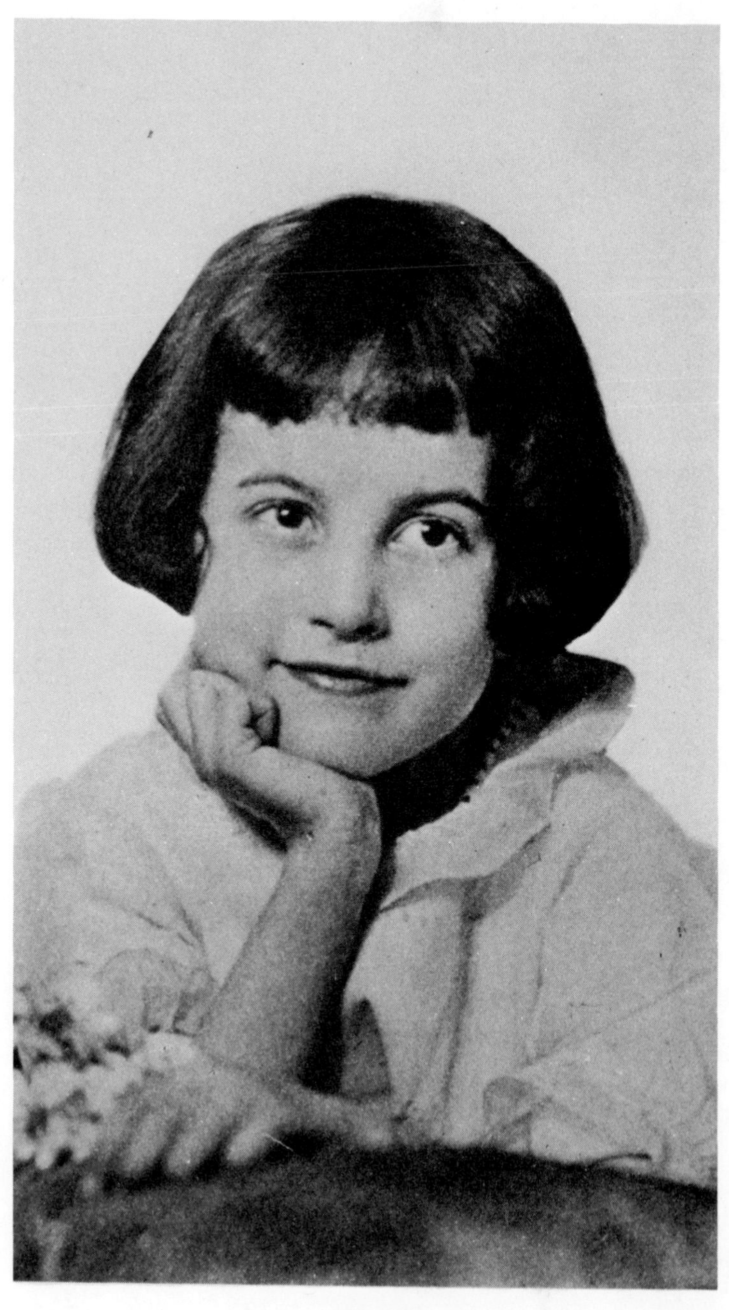

1

WHEN I WAS A CHILD, MY PARENTS WERE ALways talking about "home." They meant America, of course, which sounded so wonderful I couldn't understand why they had ever left it. Why had they traveled halfway around the world to China to have me and then just stayed on, talking about "home?" Naturally, I wanted to hear about America but I could only daydream and wait for the years to go by until we would return. In the meantime my grandmother wrote me letters. She said she wished I was there to go blackberry picking with her. Or she told me she was baking an apple pie and why wasn't I around to peel the apples? I had never picked a blackberry in my life. I had never peeled an apple. Somehow, living on the opposite side of the world as I did, I didn't feel like a *real* American.

But maybe when I was twelve years old, I told myself, I'd begin to feel like a real American. Twelve years old was the beginning of growing up, so perhaps I would change.

The day before my twelfth birthday I asked my mother what the chances were, but, as usual, she was impatient with my American feelings. "You have always been a real American," she said. She was sorting out clothes in her closet and she didn't even turn around.

"Not born and bred," I said.

"Well, being twelve isn't going to make any difference."

And she was right.

It took me a long time to feel like a real American. Even after we came back to America when I was thirteen and I began picking berries and peeling apples and roller-skating and doing all sorts of American things, I didn't feel as American as I thought I should. Not as American, I imagined, as my cousin Charlotte must feel. After all, she didn't have anything in her head but American thoughts and American pictures. Even in her dreams she would have to stay put in Washington, P.A., because that's where she'd always been.

But not me. As soon as I was asleep, off I'd rush to the Yangtse River. I didn't do anything on the river; I just looked at it, letting the orange-brown foreverness of it flow past and, it seemed, even flow through me. As hard as I was trying to grow up American, I could not let China go.

Eventually I did come to feel American, but only after I had grown up and married a born-and-bred American and had two born-and-bred American children. And most important, I could not feel that I truly belonged to my country until I had waded into history and stretched my own American experience into the past.

Still, all the time I was growing up and even after I was grown up, the Yangtse River hovered on my horizon. Wide-eyed junks stared at me as they sailed past, as if they were trying to remember who I was. When I was in high school, I wrote in my diary, "If somehow, sometime I do not go back to China, I will never forgive myself." About the same time I wrote the first poem I had ever written without rhyme. It was on a Saturday morning; I wrote it, sitting up in bed, still in my pajamas. I was excited because almost as soon as I had started I felt that I was not writing the poem at all; it was writing me. When I had finished, I took it downstairs to read to my mother, who was peeling potatoes at the kitchen sink.

I began my poem and ended it with the same line: "It will not be the same when I go back."

Somewhere between the two lines I began to cry. I was surprised at myself. I had never cried over poetry before, especially my own, which always sounded better in my head than it did after it reached the paper. This poem, however, made it right to the paper as if it had skipped the poky in-between business of writing altogether. But what surprises me now is that I said "when" I go back to China. Not "if." This was 1932 and Japan had taken over Manchuria and was threatening China. How did I know that there would even be a China to go back to? Moreover, where did I think I'd find the money to go back? This was the depression. Whenever we traveled, it was never across more than two or three states and if I was lucky enough to see an ocean, it was the Atlantic. I didn't suppose I'd ever see the Pacific Ocean again, let alone cross it. Maybe that was what made me cry: I wouldn't go back and I knew it.

I'd just have to do a good job of remembering, I told myself. And I did. Over and over again I pictured myself walking the streets of Hankow, pointing out places of interest to an imaginary friend of the future. "And that's where I went to school," I'd say, wondering if the red brick British School would look as big and hateful to me now as it did then. "And there's the Customs House," I'd say. I couldn't imagine Hankow without its Customs House tower guarding the waterfront, its clock ticking off the minutes through good times and bad.

My mother and father and I kept China alive through

the language too. Many Chinese phrases had long ago settled so comfortably into our family conversation that we never thought of using the English equivalents. "Xiaosyin," we'd say when we wanted to warn one another to be careful. "Manmande zou," my mother and I would tell my father when he was driving too fast, as he so often did. He was not a man who liked to be corrected, but he took it more easily when he was told in Chinese. And if I had a cold and was sniffling instead of blowing my nose, my mother would tell me to "kai bitzi." There were dozens of such everyday expressions that kept the two parts of my life linked together, reassuring me that my childhood hadn't been just made up.

Eventually Japan did go to war with China and eventually that war became part of World War II and part of my own life. I was twenty-six and had been married to Michael Fritz five weeks when the news came. It was on a Sunday morning with the sun streaming through the window of our new apartment, making patterns on our new rose-colored couch, breaking into rainbows as it struck the crystal bowl on our coffee table. I was setting the table. I loved setting it, placing the new pink plates just so, one across from the other, lining up the silverware in the order of their duty. And then Michael turned on the radio. Japan had dropped bombs on Pearl Harbor, the radio announcer said. *Our* Pearl Harbor in Hawaii.

I let the silverware scatter on the table. "What does it mean?" I whispered.

"War," Michael said. "We're at war."

I was amazed that he could make that terrible leap so quickly. Deep down I knew he was right but I wasn't ready to believe it. Not yet. Not so soon. Of course I had been on the edge of wars before. Indeed, I had spent my childhood in a country constantly at battle, but that had been between warlords I had never seen, soldiers I didn't know. This was different. Right then the war boiled down to one person. Michael.

Two months later Michael was in uniform; our rose couch, our pink plates were stored away. Within six months we were both in San Francisco where he was stationed—for how long we didn't know. It was there that our son, David, was born and there that I saw the Pacific Ocean again. Most often I saw it from the roof of our apartment house while I was hanging the laundry out to dry. Pinning the clothes to the line, I would look at the Golden Gate, that same Golden Gate that had been my first view of America when we returned from China so many years ago. I could still feel the wonder of the hills, the *American* hills slipping into the bay, but when I looked beyond at the ocean itself, I could not follow it all the way to China. Between China and me there were troopships now and bombers. Islands that had to be fought over. From day to day I never knew when Michael might have to go. Would the war make me forget all that I'd tried to remember? Would I ever be able to find China again? Yet when I bought David his first ice cream cone, I found myself telling him that this was "bingqilin." He laughed. Why wouldn't he? The Chinese word is just right: a quick lick of a sound and then coming back, the tongue tingling for more.

Michael and I were lucky. When the war ended in 1945, we were still together on the west coast. David made a record to send to his grandparents. "War's over!" he screamed into the microphone. "War's over!" Before we left for the east, I went up to the roof for a last look at the Pacific Ocean. I closed my eyes so I could push back the horizon, push it back and back until I had crossed the International Date Line which separated the American

world from the Chinese one, holding them a day apart from each other. On I went until I came to Shanghai and then I had no trouble. In a flash I was down the six hundred and eighty miles of the Yangtse River to Hankow. And there was the Customs House tower and there was the clock, round-faced and steady, ticking away as usual. Or was it? Hankow had been bombed over and over again during the war. How did I know what was standing and what wasn't?

I opened my eyes quickly and looked at the Golden Gate; at least it was still there. I raised my hand in a kind of salute, maybe a farewell, but to what I wasn't sure. The Pacific Ocean certainly. The war too. And perhaps more.

Back home in the east, we became busy making a new life for ourselves. We added a new member to our family—Andrea, four years younger than David, named for the Andrea who had been my best friend in China. We moved to Dobbs Ferry, a village on the Hudson River twenty miles north of New York City, and I found a house and a street that were so American-looking, they might have come off a cover of *The Saturday Evening Post.* Of course this was just what I wanted. I enjoyed my children's American childhoods so much, it was hard sometimes to be a mother instead of simply a playmate. But when we went to the park beside the Hudson River, I always told my children to breathe deeply. "The river smells just like the Yangtse," I told them. I don't know why it is, but all rivers smell the same. Like the Yangtse. Once Andrea looked at me curiously.

"Do you miss the Yangtse, Mom?" she asked.

"Yes," I said, "I miss the Yangtse."

In a way my childhood seemed like a closed book now, just as China had become a closed country to Americans.

For after the war with Japan, the Chinese had gone on fighting—a civil war this time, the Nationalists under Chiang Kaishek against the Communists under Mao Zedong. And in 1949, when the Communists won, America refused to recognize Communist China and broke off diplomatic relations. Even if I'd been able to go back, I couldn't now. Yet it was strange to think that I'd been right there in the very same city when the Nationalists and Communists began having their troubles. When they first came to Hankow, they had all belonged to one big party, the Nationalists (or Guomintang), all of them out to unite China and reform it with the help of Russian advisors who had been there since the time of Sun Yatsen, the leader of the Revolutionary movement.

It certainly needed uniting. All I could remember was warlords fighting each other, winning a little, losing a little, but no one strong enough to win over the whole country. And it needed reforming. I couldn't walk to school in Hankow without passing beggars displaying their sores and their deformities, hoping for a copper or two. The begging was always more pitiful, more intense when my parents were along because, of course, they were the ones expected to have money. It was then that bands of skinny, hungry, ragged children would follow us, each one trying to outshriek the other for our attention. The poverty in both the city and the countryside was so terrible, it didn't just make you feel sorry. It made you hurt.

But the Nationalists were going to change all that even though their leader Sun Yatsen had died in 1925. In 1926 Chiang Kaishek, commander in chief of the army in Canton, began what he called his Northern Expedition to capture the large cities of China and one by one subdue the warlords or persuade them to join him. He did well.

By the end of the year Nationalist forces were in Hankow and all that area was in their hands. It was soon after this that the Communists began to see that they had basic disagreements with Chiang Kaishek. First and foremost, Chiang wanted to unite the country politically, while the Communists were anxious to promote a popular revolt among peasants and laborers. Chiang wanted to attack Shanghai; the Communists wanted to move on to Peking (now called Beijing). Moreover, the Communists didn't trust Chiang, because he made deals with conservative businessmen, both Chinese and foreign, and used their money. Nor did the Russian advisors trust him. A Russian named Michael Borodin, who lived in Hankow, was particularly antagonistic.

I remember my father pointing out Borodin's house to me and I remember wishing he'd come out that very minute so I could see him. Foreigners, who blamed Borodin for the strikes and riots in Hankow, talked about him as if he were the devil himself. Probably it was just as well that I didn't see him because I now know that he was a strong, but twinkling sort of man with a black brush of a moustache. Not at all evil-looking. I would have been disappointed.

In any case, the Party split up while I was in Hankow. Borodin went back to Russia and the Nationalists who were in authority began capturing Communist leaders and beheading them. Hundreds of them. My father never told me about all the heads sticking on the tops of poles in the center of town, but I heard.

Most Americans, however, seemed to favor Chiang Kaishek—perhaps because he was a Christian married to a Wellesley graduate from a famous Chinese family. Perhaps they knew that, unlike the Communists, he would let the foreigners stay in China, making money. Perhaps they turned to him simply because the word "Communist" tends to make Americans nervous. But as it turned out, it didn't matter which side America preferred. In the end when the two sides finally fought it out (1945–1949), Mao Zedong won and took over the country. And Chiang Kaishek fled to Taiwan, which he insisted was the "real" China.

Back in America we had of course followed the war and when it was over, we picked up what news we could. China was sealed off from the rest of the world now and news was scarce. Yet some of the reports sounded good. I remember the day when my father looked up from a newspaper. "You know," he said, "the Chinese kind of Communists may not be so bad, after all. It sounds as if they really are going to change things for the peasants."

But much of the news sounded as if it were coming from a strange country that had not only disowned me but hated me. As a child, I had been used to Chinese calling me a "foreign devil" and I couldn't blame them. I had often felt guilty being where I wasn't wanted, having so much more than the poor people. But not all Chinese had disliked us. We'd always had Chinese friends, but now when we saw pictures of crowds of Chinese, they were all carrying signs that called Americans "dogs," that said "Down with America!" It didn't look as if we could make a single friend even if we did go back. Sometimes the memory swept over me that I had a sister buried in that country. A baby sister left behind in Communist China. So far away. So lonely. How could it be? I asked myself. How could it be?

It became harder and harder to imagine China either as we'd known it or as it had become. Then one day came a piece of news that brought Hankow zooming back to life. A bridge had been built over the Yangtse between Hanyang, the city on the east of Hankow, and Wuchang, the city across the river. Imagine! my father said. A bridge! Foreigners had always insisted that a bridge could never be built across the Yangtse. The current was too swift at Hankow and the river too wide—almost a mile. The Chinese themselves had a saying: "Putting a bridge across the Yangtse is as likely to happen as having the sun shine 360 days in a row." But *Life* magazine had a picture of the bridge. There it was, solid and real; two tiers stretched from Tortoise Hill on the Hankow side to Snake Hill in Wuchang. It had white stone towers tilting up like the tip-ends of pagodas and under the bridge ran the river, orange-brown as ever.

"It's just as beautiful as the George Washington Bridge," I said.

"It's better." My father beamed as if he had built the bridge himself.

Time passed. For the most part time seems to proceed at a reasonable pace, but once you have gone through quite a bit of it and look back, it seems no more than a snap of the fingers. Our children grew up and left home; Michael retired from his work at Columbia University; my mother died; my father grew old and older, fighting old age every inch of the way. After China made friends with America again (in 1972 after President Nixon's visit), foreigners were allowed back in the country and could join conducted tours. I felt that I couldn't leave my father now, but we followed all the firsthand reports of the New China, which at first seemed to be filled with nothing but good news.

Chairman Mao had gotten rid of all the flies in China, it was said. My father whistled. "Well, that's nothing to sniff at!"

Chairman Mao had changed human behavior. Children

didn't fight anymore. People had become so honest, a foreigner couldn't even leave a stick of gum behind without someone rushing up to return it.

My father and I wondered about the reports, but most of all what my father liked to do now was go over old times. Together we'd draw maps of Hankow as we remembered it, and we practiced speaking Chinese, seeing how long we could keep a conversation going without getting stuck.

Sometimes my father remembered things I'd never heard before. One day, looking out the window of the infirmary of his retirement home, he suddenly announced, "I'll never forget the night you were born."

I kept very still. No one had ever told me about the night I'd been born.

"Your mother was very sick," he said. "She had amoebic dysentery and was afraid that this was going to affect you. The night when she went to the hospital, she was sure that something had already happened to you. It was raining that night. I had the servants carry Mother on a stretcher all the way to the hospital while I walked, holding an umbrella over her. After she was in bed, Dr. Skinner came in to examine her. When he'd finished, he told her that nothing had gone wrong. The baby was just fine.

"And you know what your mother did after he'd left?" My father chuckled. "She got out of bed and danced around the room. Danced and danced."

It was the most beautiful getting-born story I'd ever heard. And to think that I might have missed it!

The next year my father was ninety-six. He was confined to a wheelchair now and had grown quite deaf, but he continued to love life and to resent old age. When his heart finally began to give out, he wouldn't accept it.

Then one day the doctor told him that he just wasn't going to make it any longer. My father was furious. "But I'm not ready!" he cried. Those were his last words.

I wasn't ready either. Not only did I miss him but I realized that I had lost my last tie to China. All my parents' friends who had lived in China were dead now and I was not in touch with any of my old friends. I didn't even know where Andrea, my best friend, lived nor what her last name was now nor if she was still alive. If I wanted to talk about old times in Hankow, there was not one single person I could talk to. It was scary. It was as if the story I had been telling myself over and over was beginning to evaporate into thin air.

There was only one thing I could do. I could write it all down quickly before it slipped away. Once it was in black and white between the covers of a book, it would be safe. So I wrote *Homesick: My Own Story*, but when I had finished, I didn't write "The End," the way I usually do after I've put down the last word.

This wasn't the end. I knew now I had to go back to China, not only to see what, if anything, was left in Hankow from my own story but to get to know the city as it is now. And to find out if at last I could call it my hometown. I never had. When people asked me where my hometown was, I always hedged.

"Well, I was born in China," I'd say. After all, I'd been a foreigner. How could I call a place my hometown if the people who lived there considered me an outsider? An intruder. It was almost as if I didn't have a beginning.

2

I DIDN'T WANT TO GO TO CHINA ON A CONducted tour, the way most tourists have to go. I couldn't bear the idea of seeing Hankow through the windows of a bus among strangers who would talk as if Hankow were just *any* city. In order to get special permission for Michael and me to go by ourselves, I went to the embassy of the People's Republic of China in Washington, D.C., where I was lucky enough to see Mr. Ji, the number-two man, next in rank to the ambassador.

Sitting in the meeting room and drinking tea with Mr. Ji (which is how Chinese always start business), I explained that I wanted to spend three weeks in Hankow. I showed him the jacket of *Homesick*, which had just been printed. He smiled.

"You and I have had similar experiences," he said. "You spent your childhood in China, homesick for America. I spent my childhood in Manhattan, homesick for China."

He was an understanding man. I think he saw how homesickness can travel in a circle and how much I needed now to go back to where it all began.

"We'll see what we can do," he said. "But remember such business often takes a long time. Be patient."

While I was trying to be patient, I bought books and

began studying Chinese. Actually, I had spoken Chinese before English and I was mad at myself for having forgotten so much. Still, I found Chinese friends who let me practice with them, but it wasn't like talking with my father. We had talked slowly, glad to find that there were some words left, not paying attention to tones. But my friends spoke quickly, not only giving me new words but drilling me on which of the four tones to use for each one. If you say "ma," for instance, it can mean "rope" or "scold" or "mother" or "horse," depending on whether your voice goes up or down at the end, stays even all the way through, or dips in the middle.

"Pretend you are ordering breakfast," one of my Chinese friends said one day. And when I thought I had ordered orange juice and an egg, she burst out laughing. "You've ordered one hundred oranges and a bomb," she said. I practiced and practiced but I knew my Chinese would always be a foreigner's Chinese. Still, I hoped that the people in China would see how much I wanted to understand and to be understood and that somehow we'd get along.

I studied Chinese history too because I wanted to move easily back and forth in time. As a child, I'd always felt sorry for Chinese boys and girls with such a long history to learn—four thousand years of it—but when I began to read about those years, I stopped feeling sorry. With the kind of history they had, I didn't see why they'd ever need TV. So many ready-made heroes and villains! So many hair-raising adventures!

Chinese history used to be divided into dynasties, each one ruled by a different family and lasting as long as that family could hold on to its power. So there were struggles and rebellions and jealousies, good times and bad, strong emperors and weak ones. But no matter what kind they were, all emperors were called "Sons of

Heaven." They were the only ones allowed to wear yellow and the only ones who could use yellow tiles on their roofs. An official approaching an emperor on his throne had to bump his head on the floor, the number of bumps depending on the rank of the bumper. Sometimes emperors owned thousands of horses and had hundreds of wives, but in spite of their splendor, I thought being an emperor would be a scary business. They all must have known what little chance they had of dying peacefully in bed. One emperor, for instance, was beheaded, one strangled, one poisoned at a banquet given in his honor; one jumped into a flaming fire rather than be caught by his enemy, one exiled emperor died in a forest, one hanged himself from a tree, and one was struck by lightning while running away. One poor unsuspecting emperor was killed on his way to the outside toilet and after that, outside toilets were banned for emperors.

My favorite empress was the one who tied tiny silver bells to her chrysanthemum plants so they would tinkle when the breeze blew. My favorite emperor was Kang Xi who reigned from 1662 to 1722, just when America was getting its start. He was the kind of person who liked to find things out for himself. As a young man, he heard that you could study at night by the light of fireflies if you caught enough of them and put them in a bag. He tried it but it didn't work. As a ruler, he was never satisfied with just hearing how ordinary people were getting along. From time to time he would dress in old clothes and ride a black donkey through the countryside to see for himself. And he wasn't superstitious, the way so many emperors had been. Not like the Mongol emperor Kublai Khan, for instance, who used to keep a company of astrologers on his rooftop just to let him know if he should change his plans because the stars looked unlucky or because the clouds weren't quite right. No, Emperor

Kang Xi wasn't interested in that nonsense. "I just go each day," he said, "in an ordinary way, and concentrate on ruling properly."

My first peep into the world of dynasties had come about on a visit to Peking when I was eight years old. My father and I were riding beside each other in rickshas on a broad avenue past a huge oblong group of temple-like buildings. The grandest building had yellow tiles on its roof.

My father on vacation

"That is the Forbidden City," my father called.

The Forbidden City! It sounded as if it had come straight out of a fairy tale. It looked that way too.

"That's where the emperors used to live," my father explained. No one had been allowed in the Forbidden City at night, he said, except the emperor himself, his family, and those who served him. And those who came in the daytime were generally expected to arrive at dawn.

I knew there was no emperor now so I didn't see why we couldn't go in and look around, but no, it was still forbidden. Even though the dynasty (the Qing dynasty) had been overthrown, the members of the family had been allowed to keep on living there. Pu Yi, the last emperor, was sixteen years old now, my father said. Sixteen! I wondered if he had any fun under his yellow roof. What did he do all day?

I know now that Pu Yi didn't have much fun. "Each time I think of my youth," he wrote toward the end of his life, "my mind fills with a yellow mist." Not only were the glazed tiles of his roof yellow, but his sedan chairs too, his cushions, the lining of his clothes, his dishes, bedding, and even the reins of his horse. He was so special, he thought he was the only person in the world, a different breed from everyone else. "My nurse," he wrote, "was the only one who explained to me that other people were human beings as I was."

As a child, the only advantage the emperor had over other children, it seemed to me, was that when he misbehaved or had a temper tantrum (which he often did—even while he was being crowned) he was never whipped. One of his cousins was whipped in his place.

But when I was riding past the Forbidden City in 1923, Pu Yi was beyond the whipping stage. He may have been studying his English lessons. He had a British tutor now, but he only had two English books—one was a textbook, the other was *Alice in Wonderland.*

The person who really wielded power in that last dynasty was Cixi, better known as the Empress Dowager, who, from 1865 until she died in 1908, tried to have her way about everything. When anyone opposed her, she flew into a rage, baring her teeth like a snarling dog. On the same day that we rode past the Forbidden City, we went to her Summer Palace, which was open to the public. The rooms she had lived in were locked, but we wiped the dust away from the windows and looked inside. Even after all this time her bedroom had an abandoned air, as if she had never really meant to leave it at all. Most of the furniture was gone but there was still a chair in the room—broken down, not worth removing, I suppose. And on the floor leaning against a wall was a huge dusty portrait of the Empress, stiff-faced and bejeweled, her lips pressed tightly as if she were trying to hold back a snarl.

"Not much like the old days." A Chinese tourist who had joined us was laughing. "They say her pillows were stuffed with rose petals and she had bags of perfume hanging all around the satin curtains of her bed."

"Oh, tell us more," I begged.

"Well, on the table beside her bed she kept a picture of Queen Victoria," he went on. "It was as if she and this other queen were engaged in a private contest. And when Queen Victoria died, the Empress celebrated. She had outlived her rival. Now she was the only important queen in the world."

I couldn't get enough of hearing about the Empress Dowager. She was crazy about Pekingese dogs, it seemed, and when she went for a walk, her attendants followed, carrying her dogs on cushions in their arms. There was a special attendant to carry her stool, too, one for her fan, one for her water pipe. In addition, there were twelve court musicians who played tunes while they walked. She drank tea on a marble boat she had built in a lake on the palace grounds. We walked aboard the boat and I tried to imagine the Empress with her Pekingese dogs scampering around the marble deck.

"When did the Empress's dynasty fall?" I asked my father.

"1911. You just missed it. You were born four years too late."

"Well, you missed it too," I pointed out. My parents had come to China in 1913, two years too late.

"But some Chinese were still wearing queues then," he said. "And once we saw a policeman standing on a corner with a pair of scissors, cutting off every queue he saw." The Qing dynasty had been Manchus, foreigners from the north, who had conquered the Ming dynasty in 1644. And since Manchu men had worn their hair in long queues down their backs, they insisted that the Chinese wear their hair the same way. Most Chinese, glad to be rid of their foreign rulers, had already cut off their queues, but my parents were lucky enough to see some of the last queues go.

"I wished you'd picked one up from the street and saved it," I said.

I never thought to ask my parents then how the dynasty had fallen. But everything I had heard that day had been so amazing, I don't suppose I would have been surprised to learn that it had happened in Hankow and Wuchang. It certainly doesn't surprise me now. Hankow and Wuchang have been the center of many revolutions, partly because of their central location, partly perhaps because of the nature of the people. Strong-minded and outspoken, my father said. Progressive.

But all this was the past. I may have been wandering

around dynasties but I was, of course, right in Dobbs Ferry, reading, remembering, and watching the mail for word from Mr. Ji. It had been five months now since I'd seen him and my patience was getting used up. So one day I called him.

"We are having difficulties," he admitted, "but I hope there will be better news soon. Be patient."

He sounded as though he really wanted me to go back to China and that made me feel better. Meanwhile, there had been other letters in the mail reassuring me that I wasn't alone in my China story after all. People had been reading *Homesick*, and some of them, it turned out, had been born in China and had felt just the way I had as a child. I was building a web of friendships over the country, like a large family—people who shared the same memories without even knowing each other. Even more exciting was that some of them had known me and told me bits of my story that I had completely forgotten.

Nancy Littell, whom I hadn't seen since we'd played together in her mission compound, wrote that she remembered the time I had called her brother, Morris, on the phone. He hadn't been home so I had given Nancy the message, but she hadn't told him. Their phone was new, Nancy explained, and not only was she scared of it but she could hardly hear me. "The next day at school when you found out," she wrote, "my—but you were mad at me!"

Once after I gave a speech at the University of Wisconsin, a man with an English accent came up to speak to me.

"You know," he said, "I think my father delivered you when you were born."

"What's your name?" I asked.

"Neil Skinner."

Of course! Dr. Skinner's son. He certainly had delivered me; moreover, he'd taken care of me all through my childhood. How we had loved him! "If only Dr. Skinner were here!" my mother would say when anything went wrong with us after we got back to America. Yet over the years I had forgotten what Dr. Skinner looked like; but when I looked at Neil, his father stepped back into my life as if he'd never left it.

Then one day I had a letter from a stranger, Peggy Dobson, in Austin, Texas. She too had been brought up in China and had known an Edward Hall with a brother, David, and a sister, Andrea. "I remember that Andrea was very glamorous," she wrote. Wasn't the Andrea Hull in my book really Andrea Hall?

Well, she certainly was. Since I didn't know what kind of person Andrea had turned out to be, I had been afraid she might not like to see herself in a book with her real name. But now maybe I could find her through Peggy Dobson. I tracked down Andrea. She was an artist in Santa Monica, California, I discovered. Her name was Andrea Day now.

I dialed Santa Monica. The lady who answered assured me that she was indeed Andrea Day.

"This is Jean Guttery," I said. "Jean Fritz now. Jean Guttery Fritz."

"For heaven's sakes!" She was surprised all right, but somehow I couldn't find the Andrea I had known in this new voice.

"But you sound so grown-up!" I blurted.

"Well, Jean," she said, "I am sixty-nine."

I knew what a silly remark I had made, but what I wanted to know was whether Andrea had turned into the kind of grown-up who thought childhood was something left behind, just a time to remember. There are two kinds of grown-ups: some simply remember and some know that a person doesn't have to be a grown-up *or* a child. It is possible to be both at the same time, carrying the child part right along inside the grown-up self. That's the kind of person I hoped Andrea was.

She began laughing. "Do you remember how Lin Nai-Nai, your amah, and my amah used to argue about which of us was prettier?"

I didn't remember. Thinking of Andrea as I had known her, I didn't see how there could be such an argument.

"And my amah said I was prettier because I was blonde," Andrea went on, "and Lin Nai-Nai insisted that even with your dark hair you were prettier."

Dear Lin Nai-Nai. She'd stick up for me no matter what, I thought.

And dear Andrea. I could hear her old voice now. She was just the kind of person I'd hoped she'd be. And she could hardly wait to read my book about the two of us.

It was in April, eight months after my first visit with Mr. Ji, that I finally heard from him. He called me on the phone.

"We have just received permission for you and your husband to go to China," he said. It was hard to hold on to the phone, but I knew I had to listen carefully.

"You are to call the Amerasia Travel Agency," Mr. Ji said, "and ask for Mr. Patrick Woo. Tell him what you want to do and he will arrange it with the China Travel Service."

I kept thanking him and telling him how happy I was while at the same time I was gesturing wildly to Michael across the room. But just looking at me, he already knew that the news was good.

I called Mr. Woo immediately, yet it was hard to believe it was my voice setting a time schedule for me to go back to China. I had been training myself to call Chinese cities by their new names. Hankow, where I lived, had become Hankou, which is what it was originally meant to be. "Kou" means "mouth" (the character is even shaped like a mouth open in surprise) and Han is the river that enters the Yangtse just east of Hankou. Hankou, however, is only one part of the bigger city of Wuhan, which includes Wuchang on the other side of the Yangtse and Hanyang on the other side of the Han. And the Yangtse is the Chang Jiang—the Long River. So I told Mr. Woo that we would like to arrive in Hong Kong on September 10 and take an overnight train on the eleventh which would get us to Wuhan on the afternoon of the twelfth. We would like to stay until October 10.

"Fine," he said. "It is a good plan. You can send me a check which will cover all your expenses including your first and last days in Wuhan. The rest of the time you will be on your own."

I sent a check that same day, and though Michael and I wondered how we were going to explore Wuhan "on our own," we knew we could only wait and see.

Of course I talked to everyone about our plans. How could I help it? By this time many of our friends in Dobbs Ferry had already been to China with one tour group or another, and although we received much good advice, there was one woman I should have avoided. Her name was Mrs. Grayson.

"China has changed so much," she said. "I hope you won't be disappointed."

Of course it had changed. I knew that. But why should I be disappointed?

"But it's been fifty-five years since you were there, Jean. I don't see how you can expect to recognize anything."

"I'm not going just to recognize," I snapped. "I'm

going to find out. To see for myself." I decided never to mention China to Mrs. Grayson again.

Still, I couldn't help worrying about the Chinese people themselves. It was true that Mao Zedong had made great improvements. He had built bridges and roads and dikes; he had given the Chinese better health care. And, by turning out foreigners, Mao had given his people back their old sense of pride. For years Chinese reformers had been afraid that foreigners, if not checked, would simply divide China up among themselves. Not only had China been humiliated by a series of unfair treaties with foreign governments, but individuals had been humiliated by the superior way many foreigners treated them. I had seen this for myself: foreigners who snapped their fingers at Chinese as if they were calling dogs. Most important, Mao had gotten rid of greedy landlords who had made the lives of peasants so miserable. Mao had a special place in his heart for peasants, which was a good thing, since 85 percent of the population is peasants. And the peasants are the ones who feed the country.

The trouble was that Mao had expected too much of everyone. Determined to establish what he called "pure" communism, he wanted to teach people to forget old ways, to put the state before themselves, their families, before all other loyalties, all personal desires. Once people were transformed, he said, economic prosperity would follow. So he set up an enormous program of mass education. People had to attend endless meetings to learn how to think the right way. They were told to criticize themselves and each other and to memorize the sayings of Mao, which he had collected into a little red book. All over the country loudspeakers blared out slogans and patriotic songs so that if people did have private thoughts, they would hardly have time to think them.

Statue of Mao Zedong

Unfortunately, however, economic prosperity did not follow his thought reform. Peasants were discouraged. They had to work harder than they were able and all this work went to the state. They were not allowed to save anything for themselves. Of course they weren't supposed to think of themselves, but they did. And they stopped working as hard as Mao expected. As a result, there wasn't as much food produced as China needed. Some of the leaders within Mao's government felt he was going about things the wrong way. First improve the economy, they said, then worry about "pure" communism. This kind of talk infuriated Mao. This was backsliding, he said; it was disloyal and immoral and would lead them straight back on the path to greedy capitalism.

In 1965 Mao Zedong was seventy-two years old, worried that he was losing control of the Communist Party, worried that he would die before he had turned everyone into a "pure" Communist. Since Mao had been at his best as a revolutionary leader in the early days of the Party, he decided that what China needed was another revolution. The younger generation had not taken part in the early one, so he determined that they should have a revolution of their own. Since he knew many high-ranking government officials were not wholeheartedly behind him, he made sure that he had the firm support of the army. And to stop any rumors that he was growing weak in his old age, he dived into the Yangtse (the Chang Jiang) near Wuhan and swam across in what was claimed to be a record-breaking 65 minutes.

This was the beginning of what became known as the Cultural Revolution. Many who were innocent were suspected of disloyalty now, especially those who were educated, those who might think for themselves. Peasants who worked with their hands, not their heads—they should be the models for the country, Mao said. Mao's wife, Jiang Qing (who was once a movie actress), was put in charge of purifying literature, drama, the arts in general. No old operas now, no folk songs, no historical fiction. Communist heroes, Communist battles, Communist martyrs—these were the only fit subjects. Indeed, Chairman Mao ordered young people to see that society was wiped clean of the "four olds"—old ideas, old culture, old customs, old habits. Eventually Mao Zedong closed schools and assigned over a million young people to be Red Guards, to travel over the country getting rid of old ways wherever they found them.

The result was ten years of chaos. No one was safe. One of the most dearly loved of the old leaders, eighty-year-old Zhu De, was criticized because his hobby was raising orchids. A man in Wuhan was heard to say that "he'd known better times" and was sent to the country to be re-educated. College professors wearing dunce hats were paraded through the streets and publicly humiliated. The Red Guards went wild, destroying property, beating up innocent people, fighting each other. Before it was over, so many people had been persecuted, so many had died that there is no way to count them all. Some had starved, some had been beaten to death, many had committed suicide. Twenty million city people had been sent to the countryside to forget their book learning and to work with their hands.

It was hard to imagine such wide-scale terrorism. What must have happened to the spirit of the people? I asked myself. Although Mao had been dead since 1976 and his wife (who had grown increasingly powerful) and her three cronies, known as the Gang of Four, had been tried and condemned to lifelong arrest, had the people really recovered? Did they trust the present government? How much fear was left?

China had, I knew, survived many disasters in its long

history. Even Hankou, which was a relatively new city by Chinese standards. A sandbar until 1470 when the Han River suddenly shifted its course, Hankou was so young, it had no city god, no central temple, no bell tower as older cities had. What it did have was an ever-growing population. And troubles. By 1650 the people of Hankou were, according to a visitor, "jammed shoulder to shoulder." Already it had been robbed, looted, and set afire by rebel leaders. It was constantly finding itself under water. In 1840 twelve feet of water covered it. Only fourteen years later it was completely demolished by an army of long-haired rebels whose leader claimed to have received special orders from the Christian God. Calling themselves the Taipings, they shot fire-tipped arrows and spread poisonous smoke, creating such terror that eight hundred thousand people fled. Many were still away when the British arrived in 1860. As part of a treaty agreement, the British claimed the best riverfront land for themselves, although at the time ten thousand people lived there. They would be paid to move, they were told, but still they didn't like the idea. In the end, however, they were forced to go and their land became the British Concession, a special section of the city ruled by British law. Throughout its history Hankou has been knocked down and built up, knocked down and built up. After the Revolution of 1911 when the Qing dynasty was overthrown, Hankou, according to one observer, looked as if it had been hit by an earthquake. During the war with Japan it was bombed for a year before the Japanese took over; later it was bombed again when the Chinese retook it.

When the Cultural Revolution came along, Wuhan was the place that opposed the Red Guards openly. Even the local army commander was against any more disruption and joined with city workers to fight the Red Guards and their followers. Indeed, the fighting was so fierce that Mao had to send five warships up the river to keep peace.

I was reading about this latest display of Wuhan's fighting spirit when the phone rang.

It was Mr. Woo of the Amerasia Travel Agency. "I have just received a cablegram from Beijing," he said. "I'm sorry, but they cannot accommodate you after all. I'll send your money back."

I felt as if I had been reported for saying something wrong. As if I were suddenly being sent to the countryside.

"Did they say why?" I asked.

"No. It is most unusual. They gave no reason."

"Well, don't send the money back. Please talk to Mr. Ji. I'm sure there has been a mistake. Let's keep trying."

I also wrote to Mr. Ji. Then I called everyone I knew who had contacts in China. If I wasn't welcome just as a visitor, perhaps I could do something in return. Teach English. Lecture. Anything. Several people wrote letters on my behalf and I waited, not daring to hope, not willing to give up hoping.

Meanwhile, I asked one of my Chinese friends who was helping me with the language to tell me some Chinese jokes. I knew that in China northerners and southerners make jokes about each other, just as they do in America. Southern Chinese, for instance, make fun of how tall the northerners are. They have an old saying that when a northerner steps on a train, all the flies fall dead from the ceiling.

My friend chuckled. "But if you want to get a laugh," he said, "just say that you are a Hubei-lao."

Although I knew that Wuhan was in the province of Hubei, I had to ask what a "Hubei-lao" was.

"Someone born in Hubei," he explained. "All over China people joke about Hubei-laos. Even people in Hubei."

"And I'm a Hubei-lao?"

"Absolutely. One hundred percent."

I was delighted. It made me feel as if I were part of a private club, as if I belonged. "But what's so funny about Hubei people?" I wanted to know.

"Well, they have a strong, unmistakable accent that strikes some people as funny. They used to say that nothing in the sky or on earth is more fearful than a Hubei-lao speaking Mandarin, the official Chinese language."

In other words, anyone with a Hubei accent is a joke. Well, I liked finding myself as part of a joke.

"Moreover, Hubei-laos have a reputation for being crafty in an amusing way. Cunning, perhaps. There's another saying: 'Up in the sky there's the nine-headed (monster-like) bird; down on earth is the Hubei-lao.'"

"Another kind of monster?"

"That's the general idea. And no one enjoys the joke better than Hubei-laos themselves."

"Well, this Hubei-lao," I said, "better get back to Hubei soon."

It had been a month since Mr. Woo had called and I knew I might hear from him any time now. Yet when the phone rang one Saturday morning, I was somehow taken by surprise.

"Good tidings, Mrs. Fritz!" Mr. Woo's voice was triumphant. "We have received word that you are a Friend of China. You may carry out your plans as you have made them."

I had hardly replaced the receiver when the phone rang again. It was a representative from the embassy in

Washington. "We have just been informed that you are a Friend of China," he said. "Please write and tell us what you would like to do in Wuhan."

As soon as I had hung up, I ran outside where Michael was hosing down the car.

"Good tidings!" I screamed. "I am a Friend of China. We're going! We're going! I don't know how it happened, but we're going."

Michael dropped the hose and with water squirting all over, I ran into his arms. After a moment I drew back.

"Oh, Michael," I said, "you don't think I'll feel like a stranger, do you?"

3

DAVID AND ANDREA GAVE US A FAREWELL party the night before we were to leave. They were as excited about our plans as we were, so it was a happy time, very different from the farewell my parents received when they went to China in 1913. China seemed a dangerous, barbarian place in those days—at least to people in Washington, P.A. My Uncle George was so furious that my father was dragging his sister off to a heathen country that even when they were saying good-bye at the railroad station he tried to change my father's mind. My grandmother, my father's mother, was proud of my father, but still he was her only son. How could she be sure she'd ever see him again? According to my Aunt Margaret, who was eight years old at the time, my mother, overwhelmed by the pitch of feeling at the station, fainted. And when the train finally pulled out with my parents on it, my mother's sister, Etta, wrapped her arms around a telephone pole and sobbed and sobbed.

A short time before my mother died, I asked her, "When you went to China, did you go out of a sense of duty to my father or did you go for the adventure?"

My mother didn't hesitate for a minute. "Oh, I went for the adventure," she said. I was glad I'd asked.

And now Michael and I were off on our adventure. Since we had been to the west coast a number of times in recent years, the Pacific Ocean was not the landmark it had once seemed. No, I would not really feel that we'd left one side of the world for another until we had crossed the International Date Line. It was just a line drawn on a map, so I would have no way of knowing when we crossed it, but the pilot with his instruments would know. I expected him to announce it, just the way ships' captains do when they cross the equator. Then we would all celebrate our entry into the Orient and marvel how in a blink of an eye a whole day could whiz past. But the pilot didn't mention it.

When we landed in Hong Kong, however, there was no doubt. Still, beautiful as it is, Hong Kong is like an enormous International Concession built for foreigners with a large Chinatown inside it, not the China I wanted. I wasn't in the *real* China until I stepped on the train bound for Wuhan. And there on the back of every train seat was a lace antimacassar. Of course! I had forgotten. Chinese train seats had always worn lace over their shoulders as if they were dressed up to go out.

"Ha, Mrs. Grayson!" I thought. "Fifty-five years and antimacassars are still here!"

I am convinced that time doesn't really march neatly in a line from the past through the present to the future, the way we have to think of it in order to get along. It is more like my kitchen "mess" drawer, a place where I stuff odds and ends of mementos, snapshots, a seashell or two, things I have no place for but don't want to throw away. Pictures from the 1920s are mixed up with those from the 1980s, with no time gap between them. I like the jumble.

In the same way now as I looked out the window of the moving train, time simply collapsed. Had I been here fifty years ago, five hundred years ago, maybe two thousand years ago—the scene would have been the same. Peasants in wide straw hats. Blue-shirted farmers with their trousers rolled up to their knees wading in rice paddies. Lazy water buffaloes with their curling, half-moon horns, looking as if they had been designed especially for China, where gates are so often moon-shaped, roofs curved, and small bridges humped in the middle. If I went behind the scene and talked to the people, I knew they would each have stories of how times had changed. But from the train window the people seemed as if they had always been there, as if they had seen everything before—floods, revolutions, book burnings, wars. I watched a young man bicycling down a willow-lined country lane, his mother perched behind him, a basket on her lap. Passing through a village, I saw a young girl washing her hair in a pail of water.

"Oh, Michael," I said, "I'm so happy."

That night we changed trains for the sleeper that would take us the rest of the way to Wuhan. These seats too had antimacassars, and on a stand by the window were glasses, cups, tea bags, and a huge thermos bottle—bright green with pink peonies painted on it. Wherever we traveled (in our hotel rooms as well) we would find these thermos bottles filled with hot, boiled water, for it is not safe to drink water straight from the tap. There were, as there had always been, four beds to a sleeping compartment, and we found a young American woman sitting cross-legged on one. "I'm Sally," she said. She was a Harvard graduate student, specializing in Chinese and on her way to Beijing for further study. I practiced speaking Chinese with Sally, but she was so much better than I was that I let her do the talking when we talked with Chinese. I was still afraid that my language was so poor, I'd feel like an outsider.

The Chinese were curious about the foreign passengers, especially when they discovered that Sally could speak so well and that I was China-born. The next morning a large, smiling Chinese man stopped at our open doorway. When we invited him in, he sat down and explained in Chinese that he was in charge of all the railroads in that section. He talked about the famous Japanese bullet train which he had ridden and I could see how he longed for such a train to run on his tracks. The Cultural Revolution had stopped all progress, he said. It would take the Chinese a long time to catch up to the rest of the world.

He shook his head. "Ten wasted years!" he groaned. We were to hear that phrase again and again while we were in China—"ten wasted years!"

He pounded his fist on the seat. "That Gang of Four should have been shot!" he said. "I would like to have shot them myself."

I could understand some of what he said but in any case Sally interpreted. "Ask him if he himself suffered in the Cultural Revolution," I suggested.

"Of course," he replied with a short laugh. "I was sent to the countryside like everyone else. Four years." Waste, waste, waste; you could hear his sense of waste in every word. "But we'll catch up," he went on. "You'll see."

"Tell him," I said to Sally, "that the next time I come to China, I will ride his bullet train."

He grinned and made the thumbs-up sign, one which the Chinese use so often, it is almost a part of their language.

We didn't see our railroad friend again until after lunch when we were approaching Wuhan, about to cross the bridge that my father and I had seen pictured in *Life* magazine. In order to get the best view, passengers lined up in the corridor, looking out windows that faced downriver away from the city. Michael was on one side of me and the railroad man on the other. And all at once below

Bridge across the Yangtse at Wuhan

me was the river, the orange-brown river, exactly as it had always been, exactly as it had appeared in my dreams for so many years. I felt tears running down my face and when I took Michael's hand and looked at him, I saw that his eyes were wet too.

The railroad man had noticed. "She was born in Wuhan," he explained to his friends. "See how moved she is. See how she loves China." I wanted to give him his bullet train then and there.

By the time we reached the railroad station, the tears were gone; instead my long-smoldering excitement suddenly burst into flame.

"Look," I pointed out to Michael. "There's the sign. It says HANKOU." I recognized the open mouth of the character "kou." It seemed wonderful to me. Everything seemed wonderful. The people jostling each other in the station. Rushing through the streets. Hankou people. Neatly dressed. Not a ragged child among them.

A young woman from the China Travel Service who was to be our guide and interpreter found us and directed us to a waiting car.

"You are going to stay at the Shengli Hotel," she said in perfect English. "It was once a bank. Built in the 1930s. Were you here then?"

"No, I left in 1928." I was so busy looking as we made our way, honking through the busy streets, I could barely talk.

After a few minutes she glanced back at me. "Well," she said, "does Hankou seem different?"

"Better, oh, much better. It's all Chinese now as it should be. And the people do not look as poor."

But there were so many of them. The city had always been crowded, I knew that. In 1850 when only London and Paris had over a million people, Wuhan already had a million and a half. And now there were four million. Some, I could see, lived in new high-rise apartments, but many were still in little huts jammed one against the other, just as I remembered.

"It is very crowded," I said.

"Of course," she agreed. "That's China's big problem. That's why each family now is allowed to have only one child."

There are one billion people in China, I reminded myself. Every fifth person in the world is Chinese; I should never forget that. It makes government difficult, feeding difficult, housing difficult. It affects everything.

"How is it working out—the one child to every family?" I asked. My eyes never left the window.

She laughed. "Oh, they're all spoiled, the little ones. With their parents both at work, their grandmothers take care of them. And the grandmothers—well, they have so much love and only one child to give it to."

She was a pretty girl with shoulder-length hair, much

too young, I thought, to be married, yet as I learned later, she was twenty-five and she was married. Her husband worked in Shanghai and like so many young couples, they could only visit each other occasionally. Neither was able to get permission to change jobs and move. With so many people in the country, it was simply easier, I supposed, not to shift them around. Besides, people were expected to work where they were needed, not just where they wanted to be. The Cultural Revolution might be over, but the state still came first.

She turned to me and smiled. "Perhaps you would rather not go directly to the hotel. Is there any place you would rather go first?"

I had seen enough of Hankou to know that the maps my father had drawn were of no use. I wasn't ready to hunt down my old house. If it wasn't there, I didn't want to know it yet. And if it was, let me just happen upon it. Let it take me by surprise. Surely in three weeks I would find myself on the same street.

"I'd like to go to the riverfront," I said. I knew the wide promenade which we had called the Bund had been replaced by a dike to hold back the floods. Still, it was the first place I wanted to go.

I recognized no landmarks on the way but I could tell we were in one of the old concessions because the buildings were stone—big, square, and European-looking. Laundry hung on lines out of the windows and I guessed that many families must live in a house that in my day was meant for one family and its servants. We traveled across the city and came out at the downriver end of the waterfront road, just where I wanted to be. And yes, the Customs House was still there. I hadn't realized how much I'd wanted it to be there until I saw it. Nor how much I wanted the clock to be running. It was, faithful as ever.

Formerly the Customs House, now called the Clock Tower

"It's called the Clock Tower now," our guide informed us.

Michael and I got out of the car to take pictures. Then I turned around and looked down the length of the old Bund. A grassy, sloped dike hid the view of the river on one side; the other side was lined with towering plane trees. When I left Hankou, there had been middling-sized plane trees. Could these be the same ones grown so tall and noble? But what pleased me most was the sight of a water buffalo lolling about in the middle of the street—this street that the British had once posted with signs, "No dogs, No Chinese." I laughed out loud. The water buffalo was held on a leash by his master, who carried a black umbrella in his other hand to protect him from the sun.

We got back in the car and as we drove down the road toward the hotel, I noticed an opening in the dike with

an archway over it. At the center of the arch was a picture of Chairman Mao. We were told that the picture was in honor of the fact that Mao had ordered the construction of the dike after the flood of 1954. When I heard that the archway led to a riverfront park, of course I wanted to go in.

Inside there was a grove of trees, a jungle gym, concrete slabs on which men played cards. One man was doing a slow-motion exercise which the Chinese call Tai Qi; another man had a circle of people around him as he told stories. Michael wandered about, taking pictures, but I went straight to the mud flats which stretched down to the docks and to the river. Except for sampans (long rowing boats), all the boats were modern-looking—launches, steamers, cargo boats, tugboats, flatboats. No wide-eyed junks now. No forest of masts as there had once been (23,000 in Wuhan in 1923). But Hankou was obviously still a trading center, its river linking together three-fourths of the country.

Standing at the edge of the mud flats, I let myself sink into the scene until suddenly I felt the whole map of China around me. And I was at its very center. In the middle. I could feel the four points of the compass—north, south, east, west—radiating from where I stood. The Chinese live close to the compass, planning their gardens, building their houses with the compass always in mind. Inside the palace at the Forbidden City, for instance, all shadows point north at noon. And any emperor lucky enough to die in bed made sure he was facing south when he did it. Not even the Red Guards, I thought, could erase the points of the compass from the Chinese mind.

Nor the moon. Chinese calendars have not only the months and dates as we know them but also the dates figured according to the moon. It is this lunar or moon calendar that tells them when their festivals take place. I wished I could connect my life so closely with the life of the moon. I would like to be able to look at a full moon and know that it was the fifteenth of the month. I'd like to look at the floor of my house and tell the time by the shadows. But perhaps only people with such a long history can keep in mind their place in the universe, the way I was doing now.

I was still admiring the river, thankful that there were no foreign gunboats as there had once been, when I heard a small excited voice behind me.

"Waigwo ren! Waigwo ren!" the voice shouted. "Foreigner! Foreigner!"

Foreigner. Well, at least I wasn't a foreign devil, I thought. I turned and saw a three- or four-year-old boy in blue shorts and yellow shirt pointing at me as he ran to an older woman. His grandmother, I supposed. She was dressed the old-fashioned way in the same kind of blue cotton jacket and trousers that my amah, Lin Nai-Nai, had always worn. Younger and middle-aged women, I had noticed, seemed to wear Western dress—blouses with skirts or slacks—but at a certain age women seemed to go back to the old style. Chinese are proud to be old.

I walked toward the little boy and his grandmother. "I'm an American," I told them.

The woman smiled. "You speak Chinese!"

I hadn't been aware of it but I really had started speaking Chinese. "I speak a little," I said, "but I speak poorly."

"You speak well." Chinese are always polite.

By this time a group was gathering around me. Even with so many tourists, Chinese are still curious about foreigners; perhaps they are simply looking for clues to the outside world. But I was a Chinese-speaking foreigner, worthy of special attention.

"I was born and raised in Hankou," I told the group. "I have come back."

The grandmother repeated the news loudly as if the others couldn't hear or understand.

"We give you welcome," she said.

"Yes, welcome, welcome." The whole crowd was smiling as if they were proud of me.

"How old are you?" I was taken aback at the grandmother's question, but I would soon learn that most conversations start this way.

Not used to broadcasting my age, I spoke quietly. "Sixty-seven," I said.

"Sixty-seven!" she shouted to the crowd.

She grinned. "Your body is very good." Everyone smiled and agreed that my body was very good.

"How old are *you?*" I asked.

"Sixty-four." The grandmother seemed pleased that I had returned the question. She patted me on the arm as if we were friends.

"When did you leave China?" someone called.

"Fifty-five years ago."

There is a way the Chinese have of sucking their breath through their teeth that expresses more surprise than anything Westerners do. They all sucked.

I told them that I'd been thirteen when I left China and that my father had worked at the Y.M.C.A.

I was doing all right, I told myself. I grinned at Michael who was taking pictures of us all.

A man in the crowd pointed his chin at Michael. "Old head, how many years has he?" I couldn't help laughing. I had forgotten that white-haired men are "Old Heads" in China.

"Seventy-six," I told them.

Again they sucked, but I would have expected that. Old Head or not, Michael is always taken for younger than he is.

But we had to leave. I could see that our guide was becoming impatient, so I said good-bye.

First I stooped down to the level of the little boy who had first spotted me.

"I may be a foreigner," I told him, "but remember I am also a Hubei-lao."

The crowd burst out laughing, just as my friend in America said they would.

"We are all Hubei-laos," a man called as I left.

Getting back in the car, Michael squeezed my hand. "Happy?" he asked.

I nodded.

"Feel like a stranger?"

"I can't tell yet. I'm still just trying to believe it."

We found our room in the hotel to be comfortable, much the same as any room in a not-too-new American hotel except for the green thermos bottle and the blankets which were like giant pink beach towels. We were so tired, we went to bed soon after supper.

I awoke with a jolt the next morning as if my mind were shaking me awake to remind me where I was.

It wasn't quite daylight yet and I decided to lie still and listen to Hankou wake up. The first sound of life was a rooster crowing. It had always been the first sound. Even in the middle of the city people kept chickens; I had seen them the day before, scurrying around the narrow, hut-lined alleys, running in and out of open doorways.

The sky at the window was turning gray when a small, high-pitched voice floated up to the room. "Yi, er, san; one, two, three." A child was practicing his numbers as his mother, or father perhaps, walked him to his grandmother's for the day. "Yi, er, san." Every morning started the same way. Some days the child got to five or six, but I never knew how far he could count, for he passed out of hearing before he had finished.

Gradually now other noises took over. I could feel the city gathering together its energies. For Hankou is a city athrob with life, intense with purpose. Once the city gets going, horns honk, trains whistle, bicycle bells ring, boats blow at each other. Cars are especially impatient. "Move over," they honk. "Get out of the way. I go first!" People pulling heavy cartloads, balancing baskets of goods on a pole over their shoulders, they all hurry.

I jumped out of bed. "Up!" I said to Michael. "Up! The day has begun in Hankou."

4

SINCE I WAS NOW CONSIDERED A FRIEND OF China, I did not have to worry about how Michael and I would get along in those three weeks on our own. The Foreign Affairs Bureau took care of us. Every morning there was a car, a chauffeur, and an interpreter at our door, and already arrangements had been made for us to visit schools, see historical places, meet writers, and go to a commune in the country.

"Anything else?" the representatives of the Foreign Affairs Bureau asked.

Well, there was something else.

"Fishing," I said.

I had always liked fishing. I had been deep-sea fishing off Nova Scotia and tuna fishing off the coast of Maine, and whenever Michael, the children, and I had spent vacations at New England seaports, we always went down to the docks in the evening to watch the fishing fleet come in. "Wuhan is famous for its fish, isn't it?"

The fishing teams went out in Wuchang's East Lake only three times a year, we were told, and we wouldn't be there at the right time. "Anyway, you're old people," our representative told us. "You mustn't plan too much."

I would get used to being told I was old. How could I

let them know that inside I was still twelve, picking up pieces of China where I'd left off and trying to put them together? Every day the city unfolded before me like a huge stage with every square inch bursting with life. Since the weather was warm, people ate on their doorsteps, cooked, did their laundry on the sidewalk, read in the shade of plane trees. Squatting on their heels, they shelled peanuts, played checkers, joked.

"They all seem so cheerful," Michael remarked.

And they did. Whenever we stopped to talk and take pictures, the people were good-natured, full of humor, glad to cooperate.

"I think it's history," I said. "Their long history is built into their bones." They look at life the way they look at seasons. Good spells and bed spells. A circle with the light side turning toward the earth, then the dark side. They had been through a long dark spell but right now the sun was shining—why not make the most of it?

Only twice were we rebuffed by strangers on the street. Both were barbers who had their chairs set up on the sidewalk for business. When we approached, they were upset. When we asked to take pictures, they waved us away, turning their backs.

History again, I suspected. In the old days barbers were considered low-class people. Perhaps some of the old shame was still there.

How, I wondered, had Mao Zedong ever thought he could erase history? In the midst of New China we kept seeing cracks where bits of Old China clung fast. In New China, for instance, girls are supposed to be the equal of boys, yet parents cannot always shake off habits just because they are ordered to. I remembered stories I had heard as a child of peasants selling girl children into slavery, stories of mothers taking girl babies into the moun-

tains and letting them die. They hadn't enough food for girls, they would say. When girls married, they went to live with their in-laws, so what good were they? Boys were the ones who took care of their parents when they grew old. They were the ones to boast about. My parents were, of course, unhappy at the way girls were so often treated; yet some of the Chinese feeling must have rubbed off on me. Secretly I wondered if my mother and father were disappointed at what I'd turned out to be, especially since I was the only grandchild and wouldn't be able to keep the Guttery name going. For a while I even wondered if boys, who seemed to have so much more freedom, actually were better. The summer when I was nine I went through a Montgomery Ward catalogue, figuring how much money I'd need to buy a whole suit of boy's clothes. Then I could run away as a boy and be boss of myself.

One college girl told us how worthless she'd been made to feel. She had two older sisters, she said, and when she was born, her grandparents were so furious, they never forgave either her mother or her. "How would you like it," she asked, "if your grandparents told you right to your face that they hated you?" Her mother had tried to make it up by giving her a boy's name and telling her she could do anything a boy could do. "And that's just what I'm doing," she said. "I'm very ambitious."

So Mao Zedong had not changed everything after all. He had not even gotten rid of flies, I noticed. I remembered the way our cook had caught flies. Flashing his hand up, he'd grabbed them right out of the air. He never failed. It was a talent some Chinese still had, I decided, as I watched waiters in our hotel pick off flies in the same way. There were fly swatters on the windowsills of the dining room but no one seemed to bother with them.

Nor had Mao done away with religion as he had claimed. After he died, the churches and temples that he'd closed opened right up again. We went to a Protestant church on a Sunday morning and I marveled at how many people were there—old people, for the most part—who had held on to their Christian religion through thick and thin. When the minister opened the Bible and began to read, faces relaxed. "In my Father's house," the minister read, "are many mansions." These people who had been crowded together in tiny rooms all their lives must find comfort in the thought of those many mansions waiting for them.

We went to a Buddhist temple, too, one that I had visited as a child. I remembered the pond with the goldfish so old they had turned white and blind. People revered these fish, for who knew who they might really be? Buddhists believe in reincarnation. After death, they say, people come back to earth in other forms—sometimes a higher form, sometimes a lower, depending on how well they did in their last life. As a girl I had always been careful not to step on an ant while on Buddhist grounds. Imagine if I'd taken away an ant's chance to rise to something better.

Inside the temple I saw a young woman with a lighted

If you can make a coin stick to the bell,
you will have good luck.

Yueh Fei's well

candle kneeling before the Goddess of Mercy. She was praying for a child, I was told. Babies are the special business of this goddess. Was the woman praying for just any child, I wondered, or was she asking for a boy?

One building I did not remember was a round cupola built over a well. "What's that?" I asked the interpreter.

"That's a well where one of our greatest military heroes, Yueh Fei, watered his horse."

"When was that?"

"Oh, sometime in the 1100s."

"So long ago! Do people still remember him?"

"Of course. The most popular serial on the radio is the

story of Yueh Fei's life. They play it twice a day in case anyone misses it the first time."

Later when we were on our way out of China, we stopped in Hangzhou to see Yueh Fei's tomb and his temple. And, indeed, Yueh Fei is an impressive hero: all purple and gold, his statue so big it fills his whole temple. Just inside the gates to the temple grounds are two more statues—pathetic, half-clothed figures of a man and a woman kneeling behind an iron fence, their heads bowed, waiting to be punished. "We call them the rotten eggs," our interpreter told us. "They betrayed Yueh Fei and plotted to have him poisoned. People often come with switches and beat them. Spit at them too."

"Still?"

She didn't need to answer, for just then a young boy running past paused for a quick spit before going on.

Yueh Fei, I thought, might be one historic figure of

whom Mao would have approved, for if he'd wanted to, Yueh Fei could have taken the examinations which would have made him a government official and a recognized scholar. In the days of the dynasties these scholar-officials were the top class in China, the ones who ran the country and lived in luxury. Instead Yueh Fei chose to become a soldier. Since Mao had always been on guard against the return of the old scholar-official days, he would have been happy to see how popular Yueh Fei still was. The older Mao grew, the more suspicious he became of education. "The more you read," he said, "the more stupid you become." Examinations did nothing, he believed, but make some people feel superior to others, so he decided that anyone could go to college. There'd be no entrance examinations; it didn't matter what a person knew. And finally, of course, he closed schools.

The present government is more practical. It believes that people can use their brains and still be good Communists. Indeed the leaders are determined that China will be more productive, more modern, more scientific, and move ahead in the world. And to achieve this the people must be educated. Since this generation had so much of their lives wasted in the Cultural Revolution, everyone agrees that the future of China depends on the new generation. Children are the center of attention. "They are treated as the flowers of our country," a writer told me. My son, David, would have approved of this treatment. As a boy, he used to complain that there was a Mother's Day and a Father's Day in America. How come there wasn't a Children's Day? he would ask. Well, in China, there is a Children's Day. It comes on the first day of June and all children are given free movie tickets and taken on excursions.

Yet sometimes it seemed to me that every day is Children's Day in China. What could be more special for

children than to have a building of their own for after-school activities and to have that building called the Children's Palace? Every large city has such a palace, but Wuhan's palace is the largest—over six square miles of outdoor space with tennis courts, football fields, an Olympic-size swimming pool, a gymnasium, a playground, and a lake. Inside the Palace a staff of one hundred sixty adults directs programs in drama, acrobatics, music, art, calligraphy, dancing, science. The girl who won the world championship in Ping-Pong received her training in the Wuhan Palace. One talented boxer went abroad on an exhibition tour. We watched a ten-year-old boy paint a picture of a rooster with such strong, sure strokes, it was as if he could feel the feathers springing from the tail. When he had finished, he gave it to me and now it is framed on the wall across from my bed so that it is the first thing I see when I wake up in the morning.

We watched a young drama student act a scene in which she portrayed grief at her mother's death; we listened to a group of teenage boys playing "Yankee Doodle" on harmonicas; and we were asked to join in singing an American song, "Come and Sit by the Fire if You Love Me." Wherever we heard singing, Chinese children sang American as well as Chinese songs—most often "Jingle Bells" and "Home on the Range," but the song we liked best was the Chinese national anthem, a rousing marching song that begins "Qilai" or "Rise up." It was sung by soldiers during the war with Japan, but during the Cultural Revolution the Chinese weren't allowed to sing it, only whistle or hum it, because the words had been written by a man whom Madame Mao disliked. Now, perhaps to make up for those lost years, it is sung with great gusto.

But if I could have been a student at the Children's Palace, I would have joined the calligraphy class. I always felt cheated that my parents did not make me learn Chinese characters, for only then can you truly enjoy the language. Instead of stringing letters together to form words, the way we do, each word is a character, and many developed from picture writing. When you see the character for "up," for instance, 上 and the one for "down," 下 you feel the upness and downness, whereas you don't in English. Again how sensible it is to place the character for "sun" next to the one for "moon" if you want the character for "bright"! 明 "Man" is two walking legs. 人 Add a line across the legs and you have the character for "big." 大 Add another line over big and you have the character for "sky." 天 So it goes.

Top: Bridge at Wuhan
Bottom: The Yangtse River (Chang Jiang)

Street life

People still do much heavy work

Top: Recess at school
Bottom: Saluting the flag at the end of the day

Top: Primary children performing a tea-picking dance
Bottom: Michael joins children in singing "Qilai"

We go to the countryside

Words have been dipped in history and come out as a combination of poetry and painting, and I'm sorry I don't know my way inside them. But since a person needs to know at least two thousand characters for normal reading, I had to ask my interpreter to do my reading for me. One day, when posters suddenly appeared on walls all over the city, I asked him what they said. Seventy-nine criminals had been shot the day before in Hubei, he told me. "What did they do?" I asked. "Very bad things," he said. I knew the posters said more than that, but since I couldn't read, I had to be satisfied with his answer.

The more I saw of children both at work and at play, the more it seemed to me that they may be the happiest people in China. For one thing, they are full of hope for the future—both the future of the country and their own future. At one school we visited, the children read essays on what they wanted to be when they grew up. One boy wanted to be a pilot; one girl a nurse; one an artist; one athletic-looking girl wanted to be a soccer player. And Fu Jie, a fourteen-year-old girl who is the pride of Wuhan, wanted to be a writer. In an international essay contest sponsored by the United Nations, Fu Jie won first place in the Asian division.

Fu Jie, like other students who show talent, will be given special training, but she will also be taught how to be a good Communist—to be self-reliant, to cooperate, to learn to use her hands as well as her brain, to follow what are called the Three Loves: love of country, love of party, love of people.

In some schools the students start off the day by reciting the school's rules. Since Chinese have always loved to make lists of rules, it does not seem strange to them to have to memorize such a list. And, indeed, the rules seemed to be rules for good behavior that children any-

Fu Jie

where might follow. Only one rule surprised me. *Don't spit.* As part of their health campaign, the government is obviously trying to break the people of their long-time habit of spitting. Not spitting for any special reason. Simply spitting. As a child, I had often tried spitting to see if it gave me as big a kick as it seemed to give our cook, but I was disappointed. I couldn't seem to get any expression into my spit.

There was no rule for belching although that was another habit I had once admired. After a meal people used to belch as a sign of politeness to show how much they had enjoyed their food. But that was not why our washerwoman belched. She belched all the time—thunderous belches that seemed to rise up and explode from the very depths of her being. Afterward she would always smile. When I asked her why she belched so much, she explained that her husband had been a very mean man and had often beaten her. Even though he was dead now, she was still filled with hate for him. She belched to bring up that hate and get rid of it. I have often wondered if she ever did get completely rid of it, but I rather hope she didn't. After all, she was a champion.

My favorite school was the Foreign Language Middle (or High) School where certain bright students are se-

lected to specialize in foreign languages. Mrs. Wang, the principal of the school, met us at the gate (where Chinese always greet their guests) and led us up several flights of stone steps to a meeting room where we were served tea. All visits begin with tea but at this visit, since the teachers and students spoke English, we needed no interpreter. But it was Mrs. Wang's warmth and enthusiasm that made this visit special. She wanted us to take part in each class instead of being merely observers as we usually were.

We spent most of the day with a group of twelve- and thirteen-year-olds who were given time just to relax and visit with us. They were full of questions. How many days a week did American children go to school? What did they do in their free time? Did I live in a comfortable home? What was New York like? Fortunately I had brought along a book of photographs taken by eighth graders in Dobbs Ferry which would answer many of their questions. There were pictures of Dobbs Ferry students in school, at home with their families, participating in Boy Scout and Girl Scout activities, playing games, taking part in sports. The Chinese crowded around, eager to see what was probably their first close-up, informal view of American young people. I gave the book to them, and in turn I came away feeling that I had made friends. I even knew some of them by the American names their teacher had given them: Mary, Dora, Eddie, Crisp (short for Christopher, we were told).

I asked if they had read any American books. Oh yes, they had read *Tom Sawyer* by Mark Twain, one of the few authors approved by the government. That was all, but of course, they are doing better than American children who know no Chinese books. Still, in their library I saw a copy of *Little House on the Prairie* and a copy of *Ency-*

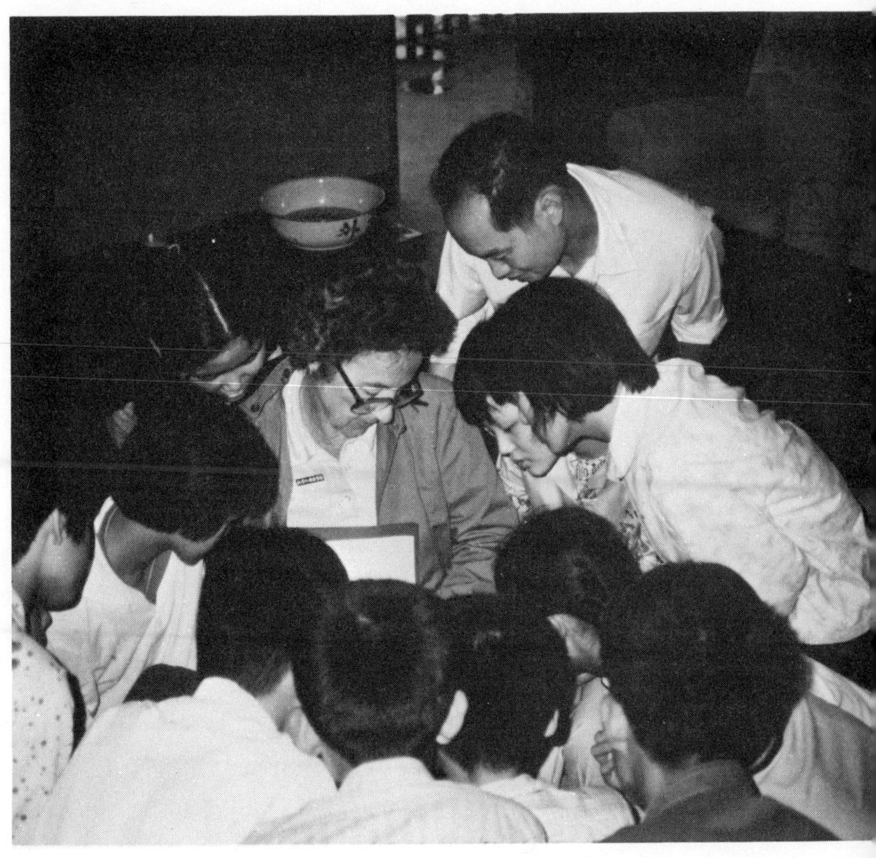

clopedia Brown. "These books are very popular in America," I said, but no one, not even the teachers, seemed to have read them. I wondered how they had reached their shelves.

We visited seven different schools during our stay, a few of which had never had foreign visitors before. At one school the children tied the same kind of bright red scarves around our necks as they wore. Now we were Young Pioneers, they told us (which is like being a Communist Scout), but we were obviously very old pioneers.

Once we had the scarves on, they began calling us Grandmother and Grandfather. I knew this was the nicest title they could give us, yet—grandparents to an entire school! I couldn't help smiling.

In only one school did I feel even a moment of uneasiness. During the tea-drinking session, the principal began talking about how at last the Chinese were masters of their own country. He was a thin, bitter-faced man who looked as if he'd had a hard life. "For so long we were dominated by foreigners," he said. "Foreigners who treated the Chinese like slaves."

And suddenly there I was, a foreign devil again. I felt as if I were all foreigners rolled into one. As if in my own lifetime I might even have fought in the Opium War of 1839, which in a way started the domination. That was when the British forced China to buy the opium that the Chinese were forbidden by law to use.

There was no use telling this man that not all foreigners treated Chinese like slaves. It wouldn't even help if I told him I was a Young Pioneer and grandmother to a whole school. No, I just looked him in the eye. "Those were terrible times," I agreed. "They should never have been. I'm glad they are over."

History again, I told myself. It was history that had shut the door between me and this school principal. In America history seemed to be something you bumped into now and again; in China it poured down on you. I had to remember that to the Chinese I would always be a foreigner. No matter how friendly they may feel, they can get into trouble if they become too friendly with a foreigner.

5

SOMETIMES I FELT THAT PERHAPS THE OLD people were the happiest. Certainly the grandmothers seemed happy, babies dangling on their knees as they gossiped together. And the old men, playing cards under the plane trees in the day, airing their birds every evening at dusk. They would swing the cages back and forth as they walked so that the birds could exercise their legs as they held tightly to their bars while a breeze fluffed up their feathers. The old men are as proud of their birds as the old women are of their grandchildren.

But only the old men in China seem to have pets, for there are no dogs or cats in cities. Not only isn't there room or food, but they are considered unhealthy to have around. Certainly the dogs I remember from my childhood in Hankou were a dirty, half-wild, mangy lot. "Wonks" we called them. Skulking, slinking, bony creatures, they looked like a framework for an animal that hadn't been worth finishing. Not like my own fat, floppy-eared dog. I called him Fido because I thought that was the kind of name a regular American girl would give her dog. But Fido may have been one of the last pet dogs in Hankou. During the bad days when the city was filled with hungry soldiers, my father had to put Fido to sleep so that the soldiers wouldn't steal him and kill him for food. My father had written to me at my friend Andrea's house in Shanghai where my mother and I had gone for safety. I remember feeling not only sad, but helpless. I felt I should *do* something. So I went to bed for a day and had Andrea's amah serve me my meals on a tray. It was the least I could do, I thought.

As for the old people now, if they are not always happy, they are at least more secure than they were. The one couple we came to know best made no secret of how

well off they were. I had asked to visit a family where three generations lived together. And we were taken to the home of Crisp, whom we had met at the Foreign Language Middle School. Since Crisp's father was in the Red Army Air Force in charge of test flights and his mother was an eye surgeon, they had better-than-average quarters. Compared to American homes, it was modest, but the three rooms at the top of a fourth-floor cement walk-up had pictures on the walls, overstuffed furniture, a vase with paper flowers—in other words, more than was absolutely necessary for living. From the beginning the grandmother took charge of the conversation. A short, round-faced, bright-eyed woman, she was so excited at having foreign visitors, she bubbled over with enthusiasm. Indeed, she hadn't been able to sleep the night before, she said, as she passed around the candied walnuts which she had prepared herself.

"I am very lucky," she told us. "When I was young, my family had nothing. No matter how hard we worked, we seldom had enough to eat. If we got sick, we couldn't pay the doctor bills. But now—" She spread out her arms. "Now you can see we have no worries. The Party takes care of old people. When we are sick, the Party pays the doctor. And I have a grandson who is going to a special foreign language school. My son-in-law tells me I shouldn't do so much for my grandson. I spoil him." She laughed as if she expected to go right on spoiling him.

Of course this is the kind of talk that the Chinese like foreigners to hear, but I knew that grandmother meant every word she said. She really was much better off than she had been in Old China. And she was proud. She had once spoken to Chairman Mao when he had visited her factory, and now see what she was doing! Entertaining foreigners! She beamed as she gave me a blue-flowered

Crisp's grandparents

silk scarf. "It is made from a mulberry tree," she said. "Put it on. You will look younger."

I put it on.

"See?" she said. "Much younger."

Her husband brought out his parakeet for us to admire, and since he and Michael were the same age, he invited him to come back for their eightieth birthdays. "We will celebrate together," he said.

It was the people between school age and retirement, the working people, whom I worried about. Not people like Mrs. Wang of the Foreign Language Middle School or the railroad man we met on the train. They had hard jobs with many frustrations, but they were doing what they wanted to do.

But there were many who were not so lucky. One evening in the hotel lobby a young man asked if he could practice speaking English with me. When I heard how well he spoke, I congratulated him.

"Where did you learn your English?" I asked.

"On the radio. The Voice of America," he said. "I listen and then I repeat what I hear to the wall. But now I have been put in a different job. I can no longer listen. I hate my job. I want to be a 'pure' interpreter."

"Couldn't you take a course in English at night someplace?"

He shook his head. "It is too late. I am thirty. It is not allowed."

A young waitress who also spoke English well told us she'd like to be a teacher, but again it was "too late." There was no chance for her to get out of the groove she had been put into.

Some of these young people had missed their only chance at education because of the Cultural Revolution; some may never have been free to choose their career. Happiness for everyone is not the goal of the government; success of the country is what matters, and indeed, before they are anything else, before they are husbands, wives, parents, workers, the Chinese are *Chinese.* They would like to feel that they are taking part in their country's progress. They want to use their abilities, to put their hearts into their work, to feel included, to be trusted. But so often they and their abilities are lost in the enormous shuffle of the country.

One evening I joined a group of young people who asked me how China seemed to me now. When I told them how far it had progressed since I'd last seen it, some were pleased. But one young girl was impatient. "Well, I wasn't here in those days," she said. "I didn't see beggars. Or ricksha pullers. All I can see is China in my lifetime, and if it is moving ahead, it is moving too slowly."

When I asked a young man how he felt life was since the Cultural Revolution, he waited a while to answer. Then he gave me only one grudging word. "Better," he said.

Perhaps the best time to have been a Communist in China, I thought, was in the early days of the Party when the idea of making over the country was new, when people could hurl themselves into action, when nothing else mattered—not even death. One day we drove past the statue of Xiang Jingyu, the first woman martyr of the Communist Party. She had been beheaded in Hankou in 1928, soon after I'd left. Of course I didn't know about her at the time, but it was strange to think that I had been in the same city while this young woman was making revolution. Just thirty-three, she was so aflame that when Chiang Kaishek's army captured her, she took it as a challenge. "Down with Chiang Kaishek!" she shouted as she was dragged to jail. Nothing dampened her spirits. In jail she fasted and sang revolutionary songs, and when she was taken out to be executed, she told her jailmates not to feel sad. In her death she was celebrating the Party. Her last words were, "The Revolution cannot be stopped." Young as she was, this tiny, determined woman surely felt her life was fulfilled. Happy? Whatever she experienced, it was beyond happiness. And in spite of the bloodshed and hardship of those days, there were many like her.

Indeed, it was this early spirit that Chairman Mao had hoped to revive in his Cultural Revolution. He himself had thrived on the excitement, the idealism, the feeling of brotherhood of those days, but however electrifying

Statue of Xiang Jingyu

revolutions are at the beginning, they cannot sustain that first passionate fervor. There comes a time when revolutionaries have to return to earth and deal with everyday realities. Apparently this was difficult for Mao Zedong. When there was no fervor, he imagined there was no loyalty. Backsliding, "revisionism," he called it. As one Chinese educator told us, "He saw revisionism where there was no revisionism."

What amazed me was that so many loyal Chinese survived the terror and the torture of the Cultural Revolution without being broken by it. One man in particular I will never forget. We met him on a train in a car full of Red Army officers. I could tell they were all officers, for their uniforms had four pockets while enlisted men's have just two. Michael and I were the only foreigners in the car and I thought perhaps I could strike up a conversation with the officer sitting across from us, but as soon as we sat down, he put his head back on the seat and seemed to go to sleep.

"He looks like an old warrior," I said to Michael. "I'd like to know his story."

But there was no chance to talk to him until after we had made a stop, when all the other officers got off. Only the "old warrior" and we were left in the car now. And immediately he woke up.

"How much farther to Hangzhou?" I asked him in Chinese.

"Not far," he answered in English. "Next stop."

I guessed that he had not wanted to use his English and appear too friendly before the other officers.

"What do you do in the army?" I asked.

"I am a surgeon." He held out his hands for us to see. Every finger was twisted out of shape, deformed. "I only teach surgery now," he said. "In the Cultural Revolution

the Red Guards took an iron bar and slammed it down on my hands until every finger was broken. 'You'll never perform another operation,' they said, and I never have. And when I asked them what crime I had committed, they said, 'You're Old China,' and they beat me and beat me."

He rubbed his stomach. "My body is no longer good, but I still teach."

"Do you have a family?" I asked.

"My wife is also a doctor," he told us, "but she is in a different part of the country. She visits me one month during the year and I visit her one month."

"That must be very hard for you," I said.

He looked surprised at my remark as if I didn't know that hardship was life. "No," he replied. "She is needed where she is. I am needed where I am."

Then suddenly he changed the subject. "You have a cold," he said.

"Yes." I had been blowing and coughing for two days.

He reached into his bag and came out with two white pills.

"What are they?" I asked.

"SMD."

That meant nothing to me and for a moment I hesitated and then was sorry that I had done so.

"I am a doctor," he said. "Do you think I would give you anything that would hurt you?"

"Of course not." I popped the pills into my mouth, knowing that I would trust my life to this man any day.

Our meeting with the surgeon actually took place after we had left Wuhan and were on our way out of China. But at this point we were still in Hankou and the next day we were to go out to the country and visit a commune. I was looking forward to this closer view of the countryside I had seen from the train window. And I was

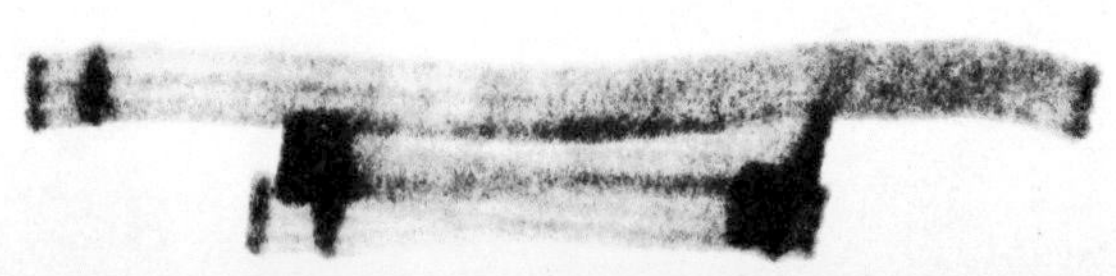

eager to find out about the peasants. After all, they were what the Revolution had been about.

It was a bright, blue-sky day when we drove to the commune, two hours away. As usual, our driver drove fast, honking constantly, forcing bicycles to the side of the road, scattering geese and chickens right and left, bringing to a halt people pulling heavy carts, balancing loads on a bamboo pole across their shoulders. Perhaps because China has so few cars, drivers are the kings of the road and driving becomes almost an act of war.

"Oh, wait, wait," I begged the driver. "I want to *see*. Can't we please go more slowly?"

I couldn't bear for the land just to slide by, for here was the China I loved most, stripped of its streets, its cement, its busy business. And I had only this one day to memorize it all—the neat green rectangles of farmland, the lotus ponds, the straw-hatted peasants harvesting

rice, the patient water buffaloes, looking as if they had personally lived through all four thousand years of history. The peasants were doing exactly what they'd been doing when I'd left them fifty-five years ago. They seemed like old friends and I couldn't help raising my hand to greet them. Sometimes they would grin and wave back; sometimes they would simply stare. And the water buffaloes! In all that time I could swear they hadn't moved. Whenever I saw one standing near the road, I asked the driver to stop so I could take a picture. I must have taken a dozen pictures when the interpreter sighed.

"But Mrs. Fritz," he said, "you can't take a picture of every buffalo in China."

"I know, I know." I tried to explain. "Don't you see—these water buffaloes will probably have to last me the rest of my life."

Judging from the peasants I saw in the field, I thought they were working as hard as they ever had. A man spreading fertilizer was using the same kind of long-handled wooden bucket that peasants had always used. But as we drew near the village where the center of the commune is located, I did notice a number of new one-room cement houses among the ramshackle huts I had remembered. Still, it was not until I met the director of the commune that I realized how much the peasants' lives had changed.

Just as cities are divided into street committees so that the Communist program can be carried out on a direct, person-to-person basis, so the countryside is divided into communes, communities of peasants who work together. The Li Ji commune that we visited has 5372 households or a total of 20,355 people who raise rice, cotton, and oilseeds.

As we drank tea, the director, a man who had been

with this commune from its beginning, described how life had improved in the last five years. Before 1978 the peasants had to turn over everything they raised to the government, he said; now they make a five-year contract with the government for a specific amount, and when they have filled their quota, they can keep the rest for themselves. They treat the land as their own.

"With this incentive," he said, "production has almost doubled. The average yearly income of each person has risen from 129 yuan (about $65) to 310 yuan ($155)." When members of a family add up their income, it is of course greater and some families make considerably more than others. Most families have bank accounts, which would have been unheard of in my day, and only last year, the director said, five hundred families had built new homes. There are 286 TV sets in the commune, 3767 radio and tape sets, 1041 bicycles, and more than 2000 sewing machines. The director was full of figures. Before Liberation (1949), for instance, 88 percent of the peasants couldn't read; now 98 percent are getting instruction.

I was impressed by the figures and also by the director, who had one of the warmest, most attractive smiles I have ever seen. He showed us a small factory where members of the commune made children's clothes. And the social center which had easy chairs, a TV, chess tables, and a library of one thousand books. Before this, he said, every evening was "just chopsticks and to bed."

Then he took us to the commune's crematory where the ashes of the dead, each in its own box, are stored in individual glass compartments along the walls. The box containing the remains of the last person to die in the commune is placed in the center of an altar with two candle-shaped lights before it, a vase of artificial flowers,

and a bowl of apples. This was certainly an example of new ways replacing old, I thought, for nothing had been more precious to Chinese peasants than the graves of their ancestors whom they worshipped.

"There is no more room on the land for graves," the director explained. "We must cultivate every inch."

"Of course," I agreed. "It is the only sensible way. The land is for the living."

After our tour the director took us to the commune guest house for lunch. Glancing at the table, I could see it was to be a feast—deviled eggs, turtle, a whole fish (head and all), cabbage, chicken and beef and pork dishes, bean curd, lotus roots (my favorite), and many dishes I didn't recognize but had learned it was better not to ask about. I just wanted to make sure that there was nothing on the table that wriggled. At one lunch a covered bowl had been set down on the table and when the cover had been removed, all the Chinese had exclaimed in delight.

"Look," they said, "they're still alive."

Yes, I could see that. They were a kind of shrimp. Crawling over each other. Antennas waving. Eyes as real as shrimp eyes can be.

Dipping their chopsticks into the bowl, the Chinese seized the squirming bodies one at a time and popped them into their mouths.

Seeing my face, the interpreter must have guessed my feelings. "You must eat at least one," he said, "for the sake of the hostess."

Well, Michael did. And I tried. I got my chopsticks as far as the bowl and then I chickened out. I could only pretend. "See?" I said. "They are fighting me. They don't like me and they won't let me get near."

Quickly I escaped to the lotus roots. I felt silly and rude and cowardly. Worst of all, I felt like a foreigner. But I could not do it.

Luckily, there was nothing alive at the commune lunch. We had a happy, laughing time, the director and eight other commune leaders seated with us at a round table overflowing with food. Whenever I could, I tried to speak Chinese, no matter how poor it was. I congratulated them on the success of their commune. I told them how happy I was to see how life had improved.

At the end of the meal, as we laid down our chopsticks, the director leaned toward me.

"You know," he said, "you have a Wuhan accent."

"Oh no. My Chinese is very bad. I speak like a foreigner."

He smiled his wonderful smile. "You have a Wuhan accent."

I was so pleased that all the way back to the city I didn't once ask the driver to slow down.

"About the Wuhan accent," I said to Michael. "Don't you suppose he was just being polite?"

"Well, if he was," Michael replied, "he knew exactly what to say."

I smiled. "He certainly did."

6

WE HAD BEEN IN HANKOU A WEEK AND A HALF now and we still had not come across my old house. We had driven along many streets in the old French Concession where my house had been, but I felt sure I hadn't passed it. My address had been #2 Rue de Paris, but people no longer knew the old names of foreign streets. Perhaps my memory was not so good after all, I thought. Or perhaps the house wasn't there. I knew that the Y.M.C.A. building where my father had worked had been bombed during the war, also the hospital where I had been born. Well, I reminded myself, I had come to China not just to recognize but to find out. I wanted to know about old times as well as new so I asked our interpreter if he knew what was the oldest piece of history in Wuhan.

"Easy," he said. "The 2400-year-old tomb of the Marquis Yi." It was dug up in 1978 about seventy-five miles from Wuhan, he told us, and the contents had been moved to a museum in Wuchang. So that's where we started the day. In the fifth century B.C.

At that time a person wasn't just stuck in a tomb and left to himself. Certainly not a marquis who expected his future life to be every bit as grand as his life on earth. To make sure, he had buried with him all that he thought he'd need or want. What he didn't think of, his friends did; his tomb was filled with gifts, each accompanied with an inscribed bamboo stick that served as a gift card. I couldn't think of a thing that had been overlooked. Seven thousand separate articles had been dug up with him: tables, armrests, cooking vessels, bowls, serving dishes, drinking containers, jade animals, imaginary birds (half deer, half bird) that were supposed to bring good luck. Some were made of gold, which was unusual for this period. Moreover, he had one whole room in his tomb filled with weapons (4500 of them), for he could not imagine life anywhere without war.

You could learn a lot about the Marquis Yi just by looking at what he took with him. He certainly liked music. One room was like a concert hall with nothing in it but musical instruments—124 different kinds. There were stone chimes, drums, zithers, reed pipes, panpipes, flutes, and, most wonderful of all, a set of sixty-five bronze bells arranged in three tiers according to size, the only such set of ancient bells to be unearthed in China. But, of course, if a man is going to have all these musical instruments, he needs people to play them. So in the coffin room there were bodies of twenty-one young women, age thirteen to twenty-five, who were expected to give him music. One must have been especially loved, for her coffin was red while the rest were black.

The Marquis Yi, however, may have been a bit pushy. According to his rank, he was allowed to display seven vessels of a special kind, but buried with him were nine vessels. By sneaking in those two extra vessels, he must have hoped to take a step up in the next world. Become a duke maybe. Still, I rather liked the forty-five-year-old Marquis and I thought it was nice that he had a pet dog which he couldn't bear to leave behind. Of course I felt sorry for the dog who had his life cut short, but there he was in a small, splendidly carved coffin right next to his master. But what really made me warm up to the Marquis was the fact that he took with him two bamboo boxes all fitted out for picnics. Any man who wants to go on picnics throughout eternity is a man I'd like.

We called on a poet next, Qu Yuan: at least we stopped to visit his statue, which stands in the midst of a chrysanthemum garden. He lived about one hundred years later than the Marquis in what was called the Warring States period when China was divided into different kingdoms, all trying to conquer each other. Qu Yuan was a high official in the Kingdom of Zhou, but when he died, unlike the Marquis, he didn't take a thing with him. He just jumped into the river and drowned. Yet the poet has survived far longer than the Marquis. Only a few people today have heard of the Marquis Yi, but most Chinese know Qu Yuan and many celebrate the anniversary of his death over two thousand years ago.

Qu Yuan, the closest advisor to the king, was so loyal, so virtuous, so patriotic that he believed in giving the king advice even when he knew his advice was unpopular and not what the king wanted to hear. Eventually, some of his rivals persuaded the king to get rid of Qu Yuan, so he was banished to the southern part of the kingdom, to the area of the Yangtse River which was considered remote and wild.

Now for the first time Qu Yuan began to write poetry. Wandering among the common folk, sitting under the moon, he poured out his despair into lines that will outlast picnic baskets. I had read some of his poetry before coming to China and from one poem alone I felt I knew him well. It is a poem addressed to his Soul, written at a time when Qu Yuan was so depressed that he was afraid

Statue of Qu Yuan

of losing the very essence of himself, the part of his life that made him who he was.

Here are a few lines:

Hide not, my Soul!
O Soul, come back again! O, do not stray!
O Soul, come back to watch the birds in flight!
O Soul, come back and end what we began!

That is a cry that rings down the centuries and one is not surprised that when his king was murdered and his capital city destroyed by a rival state, Qu Yuan drowned himself. The actual events disturbed him less than the fact that his king had become so corrupt, he was the cause of the kingdom's downfall. Morality and power, Qu Yuan mourned, seemed unable to live together.

Qu Yuan is supposed to have killed himself around the fifth day of the fifth moon, which also happens to be the time when Chinese celebrate the coming of spring, the time when they have finished planting and transplanting their rice. So the celebration of Qu Yuan has become linked with the age-old ritual of driving off evil river gods to ensure rain for spring crops. Every year along the rivers of central China and the coast of southern China, boats decked out with dragon heads hold regattas. In memory of Qu Yuan, people throw triangles of sticky rice wrapped in leaves into the water, and if this also keeps away evil spirits, so much the better. Sometimes the rice triangles are tied up with five different colors of thread which symbolize eternal life. During the regatta, crew members of the dragon boats call back Qu Yuan's soul, singing and drumming.

How I envy the way the Chinese tie their lives so closely to the moon and the seasons! When the first day of spring arrives in America, what do we do? Well, Michael may glance at the calendar and say, "Hey, today is the first day of spring." And I'll say, "Well, so it is." But we don't rush down to the Hudson River and launch any dragon boats. It seems a shame.

There are more seasonal festivals in the fall. Just the week before, the mid-autumn festival had been celebrated when, according to tradition, the dragons of fertility are bidden farewell as they return to the river to hibernate for the winter. This celebration is less dramatic than the dragon boat one; still, it is a holiday and red lanterns are hung out all over the city. In front of our hotel there were strings of bobbing lanterns. Like our Thanksgiving, this is a time for family feasts. The special dish on this occasion is the moon cake—small, round pastry cakes with different kinds of filling. We had lunch that day with a group of children's writers who gave Michael and me a big tin of moon cakes. They were delicious, especially the ones filled with sesame seeds.

I wondered if Qu Yuan and the Marquis Yi would be surprised to know what had happened to them in the course of history. But that's the way history is. Unpredictable. Heaving up some bits of the past, tossing away others. History won't even lie still long enough to let events be carried out in any kind of planned order. Take the Revolution of 1911. What a mixed-up piece of history that is! The Revolution, aimed at overthrowing the dynasty, wasn't supposed to take place until December, but on October 9 some bombs accidentally exploded at the Revolutionary headquarters in Hankou. The Revolutionary soldiers had either to go ahead quickly with their revolution or to run away before they were caught.

They didn't even have a proper military commander. Sun Yatsen, the leader, was in America trying to raise money. Huang Xing, next in command, had not yet arrived. Still, they went ahead. But not smoothly. The man who was supposed to give the signal for the action to start didn't get around to doing it. Nevertheless, before noon on October 11 the Revolutionary Army had taken Wuchang, stopping the Manchus (the Imperial Army) at what has become known as Uprising Gate.

When I was a girl, the city of Wuchang across the Yangtse was still surrounded by its wall and ten handsome arched gates. Now only Uprising Gate remains, a monument to the Revolution. Actually, the Revolutionary Army fought successfully for only a few days before reinforcements from the Imperial Army arrived. Then not even Huang Xing, who arrived in Hankou on October 28 disguised as a Red Cross worker, was able to turn defeat back to victory. Fighting in the streets went on for another month with a total of ten thousand soldiers killed. Yet as it turned out, it didn't matter who won or lost these battles. Word of the action at Uprising Gate

Uprising Gate

had so inspired the rest of the country that, one after another, fifteen provinces seceded from the empire. And that was the end of the last dynasty.

After going through the museum at Uprising Gate, our interpreter asked if we'd like to see the statue of Huang Xing.

Yes, I said, I would. I was interested in this military man who, except in battle, always wore a frock coat and whose favorite pastime was drawing. As a young teacher, he had during his daytime classes drawn vegetables and fruit on the blackboard for his students to copy. At his evening sessions he drew diagrams of military tactics for his followers. Eight times from 1907 to 1911 he had tried to bring about revolution, but each time he had failed. The Imperial government had put a price on his head and just six months before the event at Uprising Gate, he'd had two fingers shot off. Huang Xing was such a determined revolutionary that it is no wonder that his soldiers loved him. When he arrived in Hankou in October 1911, it is said that the army went wild, greeting him as if he were a "general from heaven."

His statue stands at the bottom of a very steep flight of steps. I could see him from the back, neatly dressed in his frock coat, but I was suddenly too tired to go down all those steps to see him from the front. Instead, Michael went down with his camera so I could look at his picture later.

"What did he look like?" I asked Michael when he returned.

"As if he were going to an opera."

"Were two fingers missing from his hand?"

"I didn't notice." As it turned out, his hands didn't show up clearly in the picture, so I suppose I'll never know if his fingers were all there or not.

When we got back to the car I told the driver I thought I'd had enough sight-seeing for the day. "Let's go back to the hotel," I said.

I had become fond of our driver who was always kind and gentle except when he was behind the wheel. "You are tired," he said. "And old," his eyes added. "Shall we take the river road back as usual?"

Always I asked to drive back to the hotel on the road that had once been the Bund. When we came to the park where we'd stopped the first day, I would jump out and walk down to the river for a quick look.

"Not today," I said. "Any road you want to take will be all right."

Knowing that I was tired, the driver kept his foot on the accelerator and his hand on the horn. On the bridge the traffic is always heavy—trucks, carts, bicycles, but it was the bicycles that annoyed the driver. Whenever a bicycle got in his way or even swerved near the car, he would stick his head out the window.

"Shoche!" he would yell angrily. Just the one word. It sounded so nasty, I thought it must be a swear word, a new one for me. As a child, I had picked up a lot of swear words from the servants and although I had forgotten other Chinese words, I had never forgotten one of these. But on this trip to China I had heard no swearing at all. Perhaps the Communists had changed all the words. Just as they had changed the names of rivers and cities. Just as they had decided that husbands and wives should only be called "loved ones" from now on.

But "shoche!" It was such a satisfying explosion of sound, I thought I'd enjoy using it when I burned the peas.

"What does it mean?" I asked the interpreter.

He laughed. "Xia che. It means 'Get off your bike.'"

Was that all? I could take apart the sounds now and I understood. *Xia* means "down." *Che* is short for "bicycle" or any kind of vehicle. The interpreter explained that there's a law that says you have to get off your bike as soon as the bridge slopes down. Well, it was disappointing.

Once we were off the bridge, we turned up a one-way street parallel to the river street we normally took. I hadn't been on it before, yet it looked strangely familiar. Surely I had been here before.

Then suddenly I saw it. My house.

"Stop!" I cried. "Oh, stop! There's my house!"

It looked exactly the same. The wall and iron gate were gone but I hardly missed them. The house was just as I'd left it. The big front door was still red.

I jumped out of the car, Michael behind me. Somehow I wanted to explain to the present occupants who I was without my words traveling secondhand through the interpreter, so I suggested that he wait in the car. Then I went to the front door and knocked.

A nice-looking man of about thirty-five answered my knock, and I told him I had once lived in this house. Oh, I had practiced just how I would say it. Over and over again in America I had practiced. And now as I repeated the lines, I felt like a character in a fairy story who has at last found the missing treasure.

Before I had even finished my speech, the man called to his sister to put the kettle on for tea. Then he flung open the door.

Over the years I had mentally gone over each room in my house but I had never given the hallway much thought. But unlike the rooms which were filled with the possessions of other people, the hallway was bare. It might still have been my hallway and I might just have come from school.

And the staircase. I couldn't take my eyes off the staircase. It was those very steps, I told myself, that I had run up and down so many times. My father too. He always took steps two at a time. And the banister. The hands of all my family had held on to that banister. The fingerprints were invisible, but they were still there. And Andrea's. And those of my amah, Lin Nai-Nai, who had to hold on tightly because it was hard to climb steps with bound feet. Moreover, I had slid down that banister. Yes, whenever my mother was away, I slid. Lin Nai-Nai knew I wasn't allowed to, yet she would never tell. She would just stand at the bottom to catch me in case I fell.

For a moment I couldn't move. The past had swallowed me up.

"That staircase!" I whispered.

When I found my breath, I asked if the little cubbyhole was still under the staircase.

Yes, it was. That cubbyhole had been my favorite hiding place when I played hide-and-seek. It had been my retreat when I was mad at my mother. My private spot. A place I could go if I felt a poem coming on. And it was still there!

By this time the man who had met us at the door had introduced himself. He was Mr. Zhang, a high school teacher, and he knew some English. He and his wife and son lived in our old living room; his sister and her family lived in our dining room, and across the hall his parents lived in my father's study. Upstairs, the bedrooms were occupied by various uncles and aunts.

We went into his sister's quarters, our old dining room, for tea. Although there was a double bed and a crib in it now, a two-burner stove, a small table, a chest of drawers, and a few straight chairs, the room itself had not been changed. Nor, as far as I could see, had any room in the house. In spite of the crowded conditions, everything was neat and clean.

While we drank tea, the sister pointed proudly to the one thing in the room that was not just a necessity. A large colored wedding picture of her and her husband hung over the bed.

"Is the house still cold in the winter?" I asked.

"Very cold."

We talked like old friends.

When Michael and I left, Mr. Zhang and I stood together in the doorway for a moment. "What is the street called now?" I asked.

"Huang Xing Road."

With Mr. Zhang (far left) and part of his family

"You mean it's named for the Huang Xing of the 1911 Revolution?"

Mr. Zhang nodded. "It was on this street that he was met by his soldiers."

I couldn't believe it. I had lived on a historic street and no one had ever told me. The shouting soldiers, the loud welcome must have filled my bedroom, even if I wasn't there to hear it.

"Oh, I'm glad," I told Mr. Zhang. "I'm glad that happened on our street."

When I left the house I looked across to where the Union Church had once been. Yes, it was still there, but it had changed. No fancy entranceway now; no stained-glass windows. I went to the car to tell the intrepreter that I would just run across the street to see my old church.

"*That* was your church?" He seemed surprised. "It's an acrobatics school now. No need to go there. We have an appointment there tomorrow morning for a private performance.

"And you are tired," the driver reminded me.

"Not now," I said. "Oh, not now." But I got in the car and we went to the hotel.

"You see," I told Michael later, "I didn't make it all up. It wasn't a dream. I was *really* here. And I remembered it right."

"And now you're back."

"*Really* back," I agreed.

7

THE NEXT DAY I FELT LIKE AN EXCAVATOR, digging up bits and pieces of my own history. Only fifty-five years, to be sure—not long in terms of Hankou's history but pretty long in terms of my own. Before going into the Union Church, we took some more pictures of my old house and I waved to one of the aunts who was looking out my bedroom window. Even though I had not met her, she waved back with such enthusiasm, I am sure she knew who I was.

As soon as I stepped inside the Union Church, I decided that this was one place where history had done a good job. It was still recognizable as a church. The far end of the room had the same rounded wall with only the altar itself missing. But always as a child, I had entered the room reluctantly, dreading the business of sitting still through a long, boring sermon. I had felt that the room itself had disapproved of me. My Sunday school teacher, Mrs. Appie Smith—a large woman known for her loud mouth and wild hats—would turn and glare at me as I walked down the aisle. Once I had told her right out in Sunday school class that I didn't believe in hell, and after that her look seemed to say, "What right has she to be in church?"

But now there was only joy in the room. Indeed, with its high ceiling and many rafters, the room seemed designed for leaping, climbing, swinging on ropes, somersaulting, twirling in space. As we drank tea, the director explained that the students ranged in age from seven to fifteen. At the end of their training, they would join a professional troupe of acrobats which would tour the province, giving performances. But already they seemed professional to me. Twelve students, jumping one by one onto a moving bicycle to form a pyramid, circled around and around the room. Children spun plates, juggled barrels with their feet, and finally, most spectacular of all, the pagoda act was performed by a girl of not more than seven or eight whose family had been acrobats for five generations. Up, up she went from a table upended on another table until grasping the legs of the table, she stood on her hands, raising her legs up and bringing them around her shoulders. At the same time she was balancing a tall vase on her head. In the whole performance, nothing dropped, no one fell.

For the first time in this building I felt like making a joyful noise, so I clapped and clapped until my hands hurt.

Now that I knew where my house and church were, I thought I could find the British School I had attended. I gave the driver directions—now right, now left, and although I recognized no landmarks along the way, we came out right. There was no danger I wouldn't know the school when I saw it. How could I forget? Indeed, as I got out of the car, I half expected to see my old enemy, Ian Forbes, waiting to beat me up as he had every day. I had few happy memories of the place. Yes, I had enjoyed being the duchess in the school's production of *Alice in Wonderland*. And I had liked reciting poetry. Still, my teacher, Miss Williams, had had to spoil it by writing on my report card, "Jean recites well but with too much expression." When my mother had suggested that I tone down my expression, I got mad. "What does everyone want me to do?" I cried. "Mumble?"

On the side of the building, a granite stone was still marked HANKOW PRIVATE SCHOOL. I spoke to the doorkeeper. "I went to this school," I said. "What is the building used for now?"

It was a rest home for geologists. Our interpreter had to translate this answer for me and even then it seemed strange. Were geologists people who became especially tired? I wondered. But the doorkeeper said we could come in and look around.

The only thing I hadn't remembered was how the whole building was really nothing but grand staircases and wide halls. It was as if the architect thought he was building something important and then remembered that, after all, this was only a school, so he tacked on a few stingy little classrooms. I didn't have to think twice about which door led to mine. I walked right up and knocked. Two rumpled-up geologists came to the door and then scurried away as soon as they were told who I was.

Inside were two single beds draped with mosquito nets, two desks, two chairs. That was all, yet the room seemed full. How had it ever held our whole class, twelve of us, and our desks and Miss Williams too? And all our seething impatience. Actually, it was the round-faced clock on the wall that had ruled the room. From hour to hour we watched it, moving so slowly, it became an instrument not of time but of torture.

Michael took my picture on a chair in the middle of the room where my desk had once been. I smiled because it

Formerly the British School

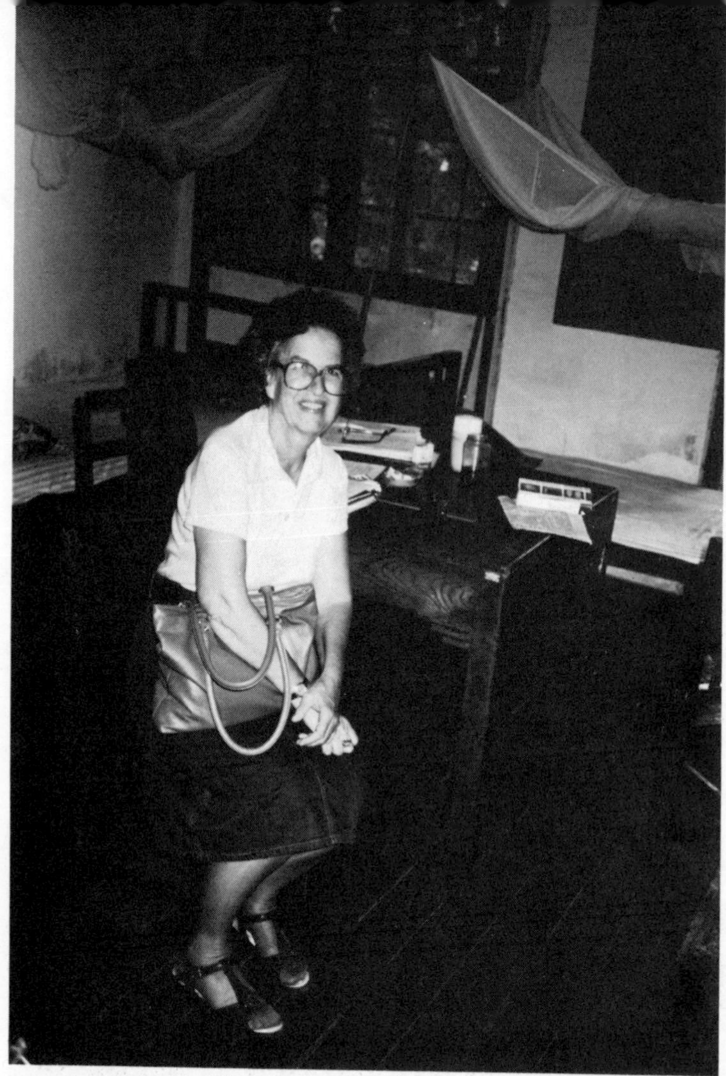

At the British School

suddenly struck me as funny that after fifty-five years I could suddenly be mad at Ian Forbes and Miss Williams all over again.

After the British School, I still had one piece of personal excavation to make. It had been on my mind ever since we'd arrived, but I'd been afraid to ask. Now I asked.

"Do you know what happened to the International Cemetery?" I asked the interpreter. "I had a sister who was buried there."

Suppose he said it was a coal dump. Or a truck yard, I thought. Then I'd be sorry I asked.

"It's a playground for children," he told me. "We can go there now."

It was a beautiful playground. A gazebo for entertainments in the middle. Swings, seesaws, jungle gyms, sandboxes, and lots of benches for tired grandmothers. Trees for shade. It was hard to believe that I had come to this very place every Memorial Day with flowers for Miriam's grave. A hushed and quiet place then; a laugh-

Children's Playground

ing, shouting place now. But I was glad. Happy children every day are better than flowers once a year. I just wished my mother and father could know.

As I looked at the playground, I thought what I'd thought so many times on this trip. China was not only outside and all around me. It was, as it had always been, inside me too. And every day the inside part was claiming more of me.

As for other personal landmarks, I knew that Andrea's house had burned down in the late 1930s. Still, I wanted to visit the area, but though we tried, we couldn't find it. Finally I told the interpreter to give up, we were obviously on a wild goose chase. Always eager to learn American expressions, the interpreter took out his little notebook and carefully wrote down "wild goose chase." Then he snapped his book shut.

"No more wild geese today," he said. "We'll go to Wuchang to the Red Chamber."

Of course I was interested. This was the building that the Revolutionary Army had used as its temporary headquarters after the 1911 Uprising. And now that I knew the history of my old street, I felt a personal stake in that revolution. If only the Uprising had held off! How I would have loved leaning out my bedroom window to watch Huang Xing walk up the street in his Red Cross disguise. I would have cheered my head off.

But when I saw the Red Chamber, it struck me as a sad place. Such a large, substantial building, it looked as if it was meant to start off a fine united government devoted to equality and justice and freedom for all. Like our Independence Hall in Philadelphia. Certainly that's what the leaders had in mind.

Sun Yatsen's statue stood in front of the building. Wearing a long Chinese coat and holding a foreign hat, he looked hopeful. Indeed, when the dynasty had been overthrown, Sun Yatsen, Huang Xing, and the other leaders had been hopeful. Most of them had traveled or studied in America, France, or Japan, and they had agreed that the new government of China should be a republican one, organized more or less on the model of America. But to succeed they needed a strong army and the support of those who might still be loyal to the old empire.

So Sun Yatsen offered the presidency of the new republic to the one man who he thought could hold the country together, Yuan Shikai, a fifty-three-year-old former general who had shown some interest in reform and self-government. He was a "man of strong shoulders," Sun said. And not one to seek power for himself.

But Sun misjudged him. Yuan Shikai had always loved to show off. As a boy, he had enjoyed scaring his tutor by painting his face with crushed fireflies so that it glowed in the dark. As a young man, he had flaunted peacock feathers in his hat. And when after a national election he was inaugurated as president on October 16, 1913, he had the ceremony held in the same palace hall where the Manchu emperors had been crowned. In his field marshal's uniform, knee-high boots, with a plume in his hat and a saber by his side, he did not look very republican.

As it turned out, Yuan Shikai had no idea of what a republican government should be. He had people executed on whim as if he were crushing fireflies. He even had executed a general who had taken a prominent part in the Uprising. When Sun Yatsen protested that there had been no trial, Yuan said he was in charge of the military. There was no need for a trial.

He was warming up to the possibilities of power. He refused to walk to a public reception on the same ground that common people used. No, he needed a carpet. To make sure it would have only his footsteps, he had it unrolled before him as he went along. Then his uniform no longer seemed grand enough, so he began wearing a long purple robe with dragon designs on it.

Finally, in December of 1915 Yuan Shikai announced that he would be crowned emperor on January 1. But even he saw that now he had gone too far. He gave up the idea and before he could think of anything else, he conveniently died.

Although there was a brief attempt at maintaining a republican government, it never really worked, and China, which for four thousand years had known only dynasties and power struggles, was in the hands of rival warlords. Yet when Sun Yatsen died in 1925, the leader of what was to be the next reform movement, the thirty-two-year-old Communist, Mao Zedong, was already organizing unions. His beginnings are also memorialized in Wuhan. Not far from the imposing Red Chamber is the field where in 1927 Mao trained peasants to fight. Barracks still stand beside the field, a peasant's straw hat hanging at the end of each bunk bed.

By the end of the day I was feeling especially proud of Wuhan and its place in Chinese history.

"So many things started here," I said to Michael.

"You, too," he said. "You started here."

I laughed. "Well, we found most of my landmarks, didn't we?"

"Did you feel sure about the cemetery? Was it where you remembered?"

I had wondered about that. It was, as I had remembered, in a central location, but it didn't seem as far away from my house as it had once seemed. We used to take rickshas when we went to it. I wished I could be sure.

"Tomorrow we have a free morning," I said. "It's not far from here. Let's go back by ourselves and look around."

After all these years, I didn't know what hint I was looking for. I didn't see how I could possibly be sure, yet I wanted to go back.

But the next morning was not a free morning after all. The telephone rang before seven o'clock.

"Mrs. Fritz," the interpreter said, "you are very lucky. We have just heard that the fishing team is going out today. We will pick you up at the hotel in an hour."

It had been hard for me to understand how a commercial fishing team could only go out three times a year, but when I saw the size of the operation, I was surprised that there were enough fish left for a team to go back for. We had been to Wuchang's East Lake before, but with its lovely park-like setting, I had thought of it only as a recreational area. Not today. A huge net had already been spread out with about thirty sampans holding it up in a circle that must have been a half-mile around. Men and women dressed in black rubber boots, pants, jackets, and hats were in the water and on the bank, slowly drawing in the net to make the circle smaller. As the net became heavy, they pulled together in rhythm.

"Yi, er, san," they chanted. "One, two, three." They would rest a moment, then heave again.

In the middle of the circle the fish, who may or may not have had experience with fishing teams, certainly knew what was going on. They were leaping into the air, churning madly just below the surface, trying to escape the net. So many leaping fish landed in sampans that the sampans were all but swamped. One after another, they were rowed back to shore to dump their flopping loads into baskets lined up on the bank. Then back they went to their stations in the gradually shrinking circle.

Michael and I were the only foreigners there and, except for our driver, interpreter, and the Deputy of the Foreign Affairs Bureau who had joined us for the day, we were the only spectators.

"What kind of fish are they?" I asked the interpreter.

"Carp."

"No Wuchang fish?" I knew that Wuchang fish, a kind of bream, is famous all over China. Indeed, Chairman Mao even wrote a poem in praise of it, but I had tasted it and had decided that it had too many bones to deserve

poetry. The interpreter reached into a sampan that was unloading, picked out a Wuchang fish, and held it up. A flat, wall-eyed creature, it didn't even deserve a picture, but I took one anyway.

For the final haul a truck with a crane arrived and took its position at the water's edge. A white umbrella was raised over a table and chair where the official record keeper, a young woman, seated herself with her abacus and her account books. Buses pulled up, and out marched a company of young, blue-uniformed marines who were to load the baskets of fish into the fifteen trucks parked on the road above us. The marines lined up, walked in formation down the slope toward the water, halted on command, and then seated themselves on the ground. I found myself suddenly smack in the middle of this company of Chinese marines. I called to Michael who was standing at the water's edge with his camera.

"Did you ever think you'd see me where I am?"

Michael laughed, snapped a picture, then went back to the fish. The marine next to me, who had been listening carefully, turned to his neighbor. "Doesn't foreign talk sound funny?" he said.

I grinned. Looking straight ahead, I spoke in Chinese. "Be careful," I said. "I can understand."

All the marines within hearing distance burst out laughing. The one next to me, seeing that I wasn't limited to funny talk, became my immediate friend and protector. I was too old to sit on the ground, he said. I should sit on his raincoat. I did. Did I want a cigarette? No, thank you. Was the Old Head my husband? Yes, he was. We exchanged stories. I was an American who had been born in China, I told him. And they were country boys. Several had never seen a foreigner before.

But at the waterfront activity was increasing, so I returned the marine's raincoat and moved down beside Michael. Part of the fishing team was now waist-deep in the water, holding a smaller net into which the crane was lowering its own net. Frantic now, fish were leaping two feet from the water, twisting in the air, crashing down on the heads of fishermen who had to fend them off. But

there was no escaping. The crane dipped down, scooped them up, and maneuvered them to a position where they could be transferred into the waiting baskets.

The Deputy of the Foreign Affairs Bureau, who had never watched a fishing team at work before, was as interested as we were. But now that he had seen how it was done from the beginning to the end, he said, we would not wait for all the fish to be brought in. He had reserved a table for lunch at a restaurant overlooking the lake. We had fried carp. I ate but tried not to think of the leaping and the twisting.

In the afternoon we went shopping. Our children, Andrea and David, had asked that I bring them each back a present that would make them think of the China they had come to love through *Homesick* and through a lifetime of listening to China stories. For David, who likes boats, I found a hand-carved wooden sampan. For Andrea, a pink jade water buffalo.

When we got back to the hotel, the interpreter reminded us that we had only three more days in Wuhan. I didn't need reminding; I knew only too well.

"Tomorrow you will have a free morning," he said. "And I have a surprise for you." He was grinning because by this time he knew me well enough to know what made me happy.

"On the last night that you are here, there will be a banquet for you. The Secretary General of the People's Government of Wuhan is giving it. Because you are Friends of China."

As soon as we were upstairs in our room, Michael put his arm around me. "How about that?" he asked.

I shook my head in wonder. "How about it!"

8

THE NEXT MORNING THERE WAS A SNAP OF fall in the air and for the first time since being in China I put on a sweater before setting out. We walked immediately to the Children's Playground. The gatekeeper, who sold admission tickets for two cents apiece, didn't want to take our money. We were foreigners, he said, Guests. No, I insisted, I was a Hubei-lao and would pay like all Hubei-laos. And I did.

Looking at the neat, orderly playground, however, I felt discouraged. Another wild goose chase, I told myself. The paths were made of large cobblestones that certainly contained no secrets. Nevertheless, I walked all around the edge of the playground, looking at the ground as I went. What kind of message could I possibly receive from the past? I asked myself. If I was playing detective, I had arrived two generations too late.

Indeed, I had almost given up when in a far dark corner I saw an old granite stone lying on its side. I stooped down. Written in English letters across the face of the stone was the name SEARS. There had been a date but it was blurred now beyond reading. I called Michael.

"It's what we've been looking for," I said. "It's a gravestone that has been cut."

So this really had been the cemetery. It was the proof I

Gazebo at Playground

needed, yet as I looked again at the playground, I saw that all the benches were made of similar granite stones set on two concrete supports. I went to a bench and ran my hand along the underside. Yes, I could feel letters.

By this time the Chinese in the area, obviously curious, had gathered around me. I wanted to tell them about my discovery but I didn't know if I could find the words. I didn't know how to say "cemetery"; I didn't

know the word for "grave." I just had to use any words that came to me, I decided. I spoke to a woman who was holding a chubby little boy.

"This place was once for foreigners. For dead people. Foreign dead," I said. "I think these were their stones. I had a baby sister who is here. Maybe one of these stones is hers." The words tumbled out in neither the right order nor the right tones but she understood. She explained to several men standing nearby and motioned with her hands. "Turn over the benches," she said.

They were heavy. Two men took one end and Michael and a third man took the other. They lifted a bench seat, turned it over, laid it on the ground.

SIGVALD SOGNDA
Born October 11
DIED AT HANKOW

The date of death, the year of birth were gone.

"This was a Norwegian man," I told the Chinese.

They put the stone back, then turned over another. The writing on this was Russian.

"A Russian," I explained. "I can't read Russian."

When I suggested that this was hard work and we should stop, the Chinese said, no, they wanted to go on. They were hoping we would find the right stone, but what I was finding had suddenly become even more important to me. Here was a piece of history—Chinese as well as my own. In all the museums in Wuhan no one would find relics of the colonial period which, of course, the Chinese would prefer to forget. Nevertheless, it *was* history, and stone by stone we were meeting individuals who had been part of the Hankou experience—friends, missionaries, profiteers, businessmen, teachers, students, refugees, rogues perhaps, adventurers. There was

SIGVALD
BORN OCTOBER
SOGNDA
DIED AT HANK
BLESSED ARE TH

the stone of a British customs officer, for instance. Born in Dublin. But who was Donald Twomes, died at age twenty-two? Who was the German woman who died in 1916 and had an anchor and a heart carved on her stone? How did the man from Braintree, Massachusetts, end up in Hankou? And why were the letters on his stone so roughly carved, as if they had been scratched out with a penknife? The oldest stone was dated 1896. The latest of Frans Hanisch, died in 1938. I made a note of the name for I knew someone in America who had been in Hankou in 1938. Later I found out that Frans had been a bassoonist and had died of tuberculosis.

We didn't find my sister's stone; we didn't even turn over all the stones, but none of that mattered now. I had discovered a chunk of hidden history that belonged to me and my time. It would have to stay a secret, for I couldn't tell our interpreter or anyone at the Foreign Affairs Bureau. They'd be embarrassed that I'd found foreign gravestones turned into park benches. They wouldn't believe me if I told them that I liked the idea. And I did. All those tired grandmothers resting on left-over memories from my time!

Just thinking about the Children's Playground was a comfort, for in the last days I became more and more aware of how much there was to learn about China, how little I knew, and how time was flying, flying! Anything that connected my early life with China now made me feel as if I owned more time.

We crowded as much as we could into these days, but when we stopped at the former headquarters of the Communists' famous Eighth Route Army, I expected nothing to turn up from my younger life. After all, this was after my time, a landmark from 1938 when for nine months Hankou had been the center of China's defense against Japan. By this time the Communists and Nationalists had temporarily rejoined forces to fight Japan, and Zhou Enlai was representing the Communists on Chiang Kaishek's military council.

A young guide met us at the gate of the headquarters and, looking at our cameras, she told us that no pictures were allowed here. I knew little about this episode in history and so I listened with interest. The nights must have been especially dreadful, I thought. At every air-raid alert, the Chinese had rushed to the foreign concessions, which were considered the safest. I could picture the thousands of people huddled together on the sidewalks, cowering as the planes roared over. There were few relics in the old headquarters but many pictures.

Suddenly I stopped short. There on the wall was a large photograph of Zhou Enlai whom, of course, I recognized from newspaper pictures over the years. But next to him was an American. The round smiling face of a man I had known well, one of my father's best friends, Bishop Roots, a bishop of the Episcopalian Church.

"I knew that man," I cried. "He was our friend, Bishop Roots."

The guide read the characters beside the picture. Yes, that was his name, she agreed. She had wondered about him—who he was, what he was doing there.

I told her that I often talked to his daughter, Frances Roots Hadden, who lived in Michigan now. Her father had been a good friend of Zhou Enlai, I explained. "He was a friend of many of your leaders at that time."

The guide smiled. "If he was a friend of Premier Zhou, he must have been a very good man. You too are a friend. You may take pictures if you like."

I wasn't surprised that the guide was impressed. Premier Zhou Enlai was the most loved leader in China. He died in 1976, but you cannot mention his name today without getting a thumbs-up sign. And so by a roundabout linkage, there I was, one friend removed from the old Red Army. I had found another small thread that tied my China experiences together.

On our last day we rocketed back and forth between the centuries. From a thirteenth-century pagoda, we traveled back to a pavilion built in the fifth century to celebrate the friendship between a lute player who thought no one understood his music and a woodcutter who showed that he understood perfectly. A beautiful pavilion overlooking the river had moon gates, a tea

Moon gate at the Ancient Lute Pavilion

At the Ancient Lute Pavilion

garden, a music platform, a carved fountain. Where else in the world, I thought, would you find a spot designed to celebrate a simple friendship fifteen centuries old?

We ended the afternoon with a visit to a museum in Wuchang. In it was a room memorializing the siege of Wuchang when the Communist wing of the Nationalist army attacked the city, the last stronghold of a local warlord. The siege lasted from September 15 to October 10, 1926, and of course I had been here then. It was the closest I have ever been to war, but at the time I didn't think about which side to cheer for. All I knew was that my beloved Lin Nai-Nai's family was walled up in Wuchang and, like everyone else, running out of food. So whenever I heard shooting, whenever I heard a plane, I got mad.

I don't know why all tourist guides in China are so young. They recite what they have learned of history but have never, even in their imaginations, it seemed, stepped inside any history but their present one. Our guide here was full of figures—the size of the armies, the number of dead, and when she came to a cannon that had been fired against the city, she passed it casually.

"Oh yes," she said, "this was a small cannon that was used."

I stopped. Putting my hand on the cannon, I suddenly felt my eyes fill up.

"It was placed on the hill above Wuchang, wasn't it?"

She looked at me in surprise. "Yes. How did you know?"

"I was here. I heard it." And of course I had. Booming. Booming. Booming. But it wasn't just memory that was swelling up in me. It was a feeling that had been growing for the last few days. I'd had no words for it before, but I had them now.

China was not only, as it had always been, part of me. *I was part of China.* Of course I had only been a girl; I'd played no personal part. All the same, I'd been born in China, lived here, watched the river rise and fall, seen the moon come and go, waited out wars. I had a place, a small place in the long unwritten part of China's long history. I held tight to the cannon, knowing that I would never again have trouble answering the question "Where is your hometown?" Of course it was Wuhan. Where else would it be?

When we left the museum, I tried to tell Michael about my discovery. I knew that in a way it seemed obvious, so I wasn't sure if anyone else would understand. But like the woodcutter who listened to the lute player, Michael has an understanding heart. He knew what I meant.

I wished there were Chinese who would also understand. Yet what kind of acknowledgment did I want from them? I asked myself. I was already a Friend of China. Did I want them to tell me that now I was a very good Friend? That was silly. I put it out of my mind as we dressed for the Secretary General's banquet.

I had worried about what gift I could give the Secretary General. I knew there would be gifts. The Chinese are so generous in giving yet do not easily receive. Even our driver's five-year-old son who had accompanied us on a school holiday had trouble. I had bought him a chocolate bar at the Friendship Store which sells only to foreigners so I knew this would be a treat. But when I offered it to him, he put his hands behind his back.

"Buyau," he'd said. "I don't want it." Not until his father had told him it was all right, did he take it. I suppose people have been taught to refuse gifts from foreigners.

The same thing happened when I tried to give a bottle

My childhood home

My old church—now an acrobatic school

Old China

Women whose feet had been bound

My old church—now
an acrobatic school

Old China

Women whose feet had been bound

New China

Top: Fishing team at work
Bottom: East Lake

Top: Making friends with marines
Bottom: Ancient Lute Pavilion

Top: Children's Playground
Left: Gravestone from old International Cemetery

of wine to Mr. Zhang in my old house. Only the interpreter could convince him to accept it.

Yet that very morning the driver had given us a beautiful oil-paper Chinese umbrella as a good-bye present. I had protested. It was too much, I said. Yet he insisted. "I have to give it to you," he said. "You are two old people who have made a long journey across a wide ocean just out of love for China."

I loved the speech even more than the umbrella and of course I accepted.

Moreover, the night before when Mr. Zhang had come to the hotel to say good-bye, he gave us a framed picture of cranes resting under a cedar tree. In his house the only picture I had seen was the wedding picture of his sister and her husband. I knew what a small amount of money these people made, but I felt helpless before their generosity.

I asked our interpreter for a suggestion of what I could give the Secretary General.

"He doesn't want anything," he said.

He was no help. What I wanted was something personal, something that would show my love of China. In the end all I could think of was a copy of *Homesick*. I knew he couldn't read English, but at least he could look at the photographs, I thought, and see the younger me living in old China.

We were to eat in a private dining room on an upper floor of the hotel. When we stepped off the elevator, the Secretary General and members of the Foreign Affairs Bureau were there to meet us. The Secretary General, who was also president of a local university, was a tall, thin, handsome man dressed in an impeccably tailored gray Mao jacket. He looked kind and wise, just the way a Chinese scholar should look.

"Our dinner is to be a small family affair," he explained as he led us into the dining room. "This is the best way for friends to say good-bye."

I felt as if I had many friends—the driver, the director of the commune, Mr. Zhang, Crisp's grandmother—but for a small party the guests had been chosen well. In addition to the three men from the Foreign Affairs Bureau, there were just two guests: Mr. Chen, director of the Y.M.C.A., and Mr. Yang of the Wuhan Writers' Association. I'd had several meetings with Mr. Chen. He had told me about "Y" activities today; I had told him about the early days. As for Mr. Yang, he was the one with the worried face who had talked about how hard it was to create a "new literature." I suppose he meant one of which he could be proud and one which the government would approve and one which children would enjoy. In any case, he was, like me, a writer who couldn't help writing even though he had only two hours a day to do it—between midnight and two in the morning.

Although the party was small, the food was anything but meager: eel, seaweed soup, mandarin fish, preserved duck eggs, duck meat wrapped in pancakes, a fungus dish for dessert (sweet and delicious). Dish after dish appeared before us. I have never seen Chinese eat together without showing enjoyment, without laughter, without frequent rising to clink glasses and make toasts. I, too, should propose a toast soon, I thought, but as I looked around the table, I knew I could not say what I was feeling.

Oh, I wanted life to be kind to these people. That's what I wanted to say. I wanted the government to be steady and safe and caring. I looked at Mr. Yang's anxious face and I wished that he could have more time to write and could write as he pleased. I wished they could all speak openly. And all the young people I'd met who

felt caught in too tight a pattern—I wanted them to fulfill themselves as well as work for their country and help move it ahead. I worried about China.

But I said none of this. I stood, raised my glass, and said what also lay in my heart. I spoke of my pride in Wuhan and my happiness in seeing China's progress. I gave the Secretary General my book, which he said would go on the shelves of his college library.

In turn, he had, as I suspected, gifts for us. A brown and white porcelain vase, tall and graceful. "When you look at this," he said, "you must think of your hometown, Wuhan."

In addition, he gave me my personal "chop," a marble seal with the characters of my name on the bottom. On the top a tiny elephant trumpeted with trunk upraised. Chinese use their chop when they sign their letters, documents, paintings, and poetry. I would press mine into the jar of red paste that had come with it, then stamp the characters (Gau Qing—my maiden name) on whatever paper I wanted to sign.

Before I had a chance to express my thanks, the Secretary General said he had an announcement to make. He raised his glass to me. "I now declare that you are an honorary citizen of Wuhan."

I could scarcely take in the words, but I could see that everyone was standing and smiling at me.

I smiled back. Raising my glass high, I clinked the Secretary General's glass and in turn clinked each glass at the table.

"In all of Wuhan," I said, "you do not have a citizen, honorary or otherwise, more proud of her citizenship."

After dinner when all the good-byes had been said, I was far too stirred up to go to bed. Michael and I walked down to the river. I took my place in the middle of the compass—north, south, east, west fanning out around me. Overhead, a lopsided moon presided over China as it always had.

"There is an old Chinese saying," I told Michael. "The moon shines brightest on your hometown."

"Do you think it's true?"

"Maybe. If your hometown is Wuhan." The moon did seem extraordinarily bright as it strewed paths of gold across the orange-brown water. "But you know why? I think the moon is Chinese. It is at home here. An old,

old friend of the people." Happy as I was, I heard myself sigh.

"You're going to be sorry to leave, aren't you?" Michael asked.

"Yes, I hate to leave China," I admitted. "It hasn't been long enough."

Still, when I thought of America on the other side of the world, I knew I wouldn't be sorry to be back. It had taken me a long time to make America feel like home. Besides, I had work to do.

As soon as I got back, I had to start writing. I wouldn't rest until I had my China homecoming down on paper. Safe between the covers of a book. And when I'd finished writing, I'd stamp the paper with my own seal. Just as any Chinese would do at the end of a story.

NOTES FROM THE AUTHOR

A note about the spelling of Chinese names and words: I have used what the Chinese call the "pinyin" system with English letters representing Chinese sounds. This system was officially adopted by the People's Republic of China in 1958. The main points to remember are: *q* is used for the *ch* sound; *x* for *sh: zh* for *j: c* for *ts*.

Page 9. Manchuria was formerly a foreign country, the home of the Manchus who conquered China in 1644. At that time Manchuria became a province of China. When the Japanese occupied it at the end of 1931, they renamed it Manchukuo. This was, as many people suspected, the first step of Japan's invasion of China.

Page 14. The Nationalists were the party founded by Sun Yatsen, and when he died in 1925, Chiang Kaishek became the leader. The Communists had formed their own party in 1921 but had been persuaded to join the Nationalists for their Northern Expedition. They were only a small percentage of the Nationalist Party, but one wing of the Nationalists tended to be sympathetic with them.

Page 15. After the war with Japan (1937–1945), the Nationalists and Communists fought each other (1945–1949) for control of China.

Page 25. Pu Yi, the boy emperor, continued to have a sad life. In November 1924, he was driven out of the Forbidden City by a warlord. When Japan took Manchuria (renaming it Manchukuo) in November 1931, Pu Yi was made the emperor but was treated more like a prisoner. In 1945 he was captured by the Russians and spent five years in Russia. He died in the People's Republic of China, serving as a clerk, although he called himself "a literary and historical worker."

Page 27. My parents did have some remnants of the Qing dynasty. In our "Chinese" trunk in the attic are several "mandarin squares," embroidered squares that officials wore on the front of their robes to show their rank. The ones we have are embroidered with the pictures of two cranes, the sign of the highest-ranking official. After the fall of the dynasty, the old court officials must have sold their squares.

Page 34. In 1928 over half the peasants were tenants of landlords who took half of what the peasants made. In order to get through the year, peasants had to borrow money and pay an interest rate of 30 percent. In addition, there were taxes to pay to the central government as well as to local warlords.

Page 45. "Shengli" means "victory."

Page 70. The Opium War. The British found that selling opium from their colony in India was extremely profitable, but they said it would be immoral to sell it to their own country, so they concentrated on China, with whom they wished to trade. China said it didn't need anything or want anything produced from the West, but in spite of the fact that opium smoking had been illegal in China since 1729, the Chinese did buy it and they did smoke it. When the Chinese government confiscated shipments, the British used this as an excuse to start the Opium War of 1839–1842. The treaty to end the war (which the British won) was one of many "unequal treaties." It allowed British merchants to create "treaty ports" in China in which foreigners were given special trading privileges and became subject not to the Chinese law, only to the laws of their own countries. Almost every foreign country, including America, became involved in the opium trade.

In the late nineteenth century foreign powers took over various naval bases. From time to time the Chinese did try to get rid of foreign powers—most dramatically in 1900 when an antiforeign organization called the Boxers besieged the foreigners in Beijing. After a month an international military force marched into Beijing and put an end to the siege. But China had to pay the foreign powers $333 million and they had to allow foreign troops to be stationed in Beijing.

Many foreigners, however, opposed the dominating and degrading attitudes of their governments. There were missionaries who respected Chinese culture and who brought, along with their religion, opportunities for education and improved health care that were not available in China at the time. Bonds of real friendship between some Chinese and foreigners helped to counterbalance the terrible advantage of China that foreign business and governments were taking.

Page 73. Andrea and her family had moved to Shanghai.

Page 77. The statue of Xiang Jingyu shows a woman with short bobbed hair, which was the way all revolutionary women showed their political loyalty. Indeed, some of these women were so determined that all Chinese women should declare their equality with men that they went into peasant villages and sometimes forcefully cut off women's long hair.

Page 90. Chrysanthemums are the symbol of long life because they are the flower that is said to age most gracefully. In order to ensure a long life, people were traditionally supposed to pick chrysanthemums on the ninth day of the ninth moon. The word for nine, "jiu," is the same as the word for long life and is considered a lucky number.

Page 92. Over the years the poet Qu Yuan has been a hero for different reasons. Because Qu Yuan became a friend of common people during his exile, Communists consider his life to be a reflection of the conflict between the people and the feudal lords. Communists say that it is not heroes who create history but history which creates heroes.

Page 95. The fifteen provinces that seceded were out of a total of eighteen provinces.

Page 95. On October 10, 1916, when the fifth anniversary of the revolution at Uprising Gate was to be celebrated, Huang Xing fell ill. He died on October 31 at the age of forty-two.

Page 110. It is not too surprising that a republican form of government was not established. Not only had the Chinese no leader strong enough, they had no tradition except to rule and be ruled. Nor did they have a system of laws sophisticated enough to ensure the success of a republican government. The Chinese nation had been held together not by laws but by moral rules handed down through the generations. The family was the central unit. The head of the family had the responsibility for handing down the right rules for living to the younger generation. (Wisdom was associated with age.) At the head of the whole nation was the "Son of Heaven," whose life was supposed to set an example to the country. There was no real middle class. Only the scholar-officials at one end of the scale, who did not care to change their way of life, and the peasants at the other end, who had no power to change theirs. And the army, consisting now of warlords fighting each other.

The Communist Party was formed in 1921, partly in response to another "unfair treaty"—the Treaty of Versailles, which ended World War I. In this treaty part of the province of Shandong, which had become a "sphere of influence" for Germany, was handed over to Japan instead of being returned to China. China did not sign the treaty.

In 1925 Mao Zedong was one of many Communist reformists. In 1934 the Communist Party, divided and badly organized, had to escape Chiang Kaishek and the Nationalists. On October 16, 1934, 100,000 men and women started the famous Long March, a year-long, six-thousand-mile march from south-central China to Yenan in the north. It was during this historic and hazardous march that Mao Zedong emerged as leader of the Party.

Pages 123–124. This was at the time of Chiang Kaishek's famous Northern Expedition (mentioned earlier) and before the Nationalists and the Communists had split.

Page 133. When we left Hankou, we had a brief trip before actually leaving the country. We took a plane to Chongqing, then a boat down the river through the beautiful Yangtse gorges. Here we saw the junks I had missed in Wuhan. After stopping off in Nanjing and Hangzhou, we left Shanghai for Tokyo. And then home.

BRIEF OUTLINE OF CHINESE HISTORY

21st century BC to 16th century BC	Xia Dynasty
16th century BC to 1066 BC	Shang Dynasty
1066 BC to 221 BC	Zhou Dynasty
403 to 221 BC	Warring States Period
221 to 206 BC	Qin Dynasty Great Wall Built
206 BC to AD 220	Han Dynasty
220 to 439	Six Dynasties
386 to 581	Southern and Northern Dynasties
581 to 618	Sui Dynasty
618 to 907	Tang Dynasty
907 to 979	Five Dynasties and Ten Kingdoms Period
960 to 1279	Song Dynasty (distinguished for literature, philosophy, invention of moveable type, gunpowder, magnetic compass)
907 to 1125	Liao Dynasty
1032 to 1227	Western Xia Dynasty
1115 to 1234	Jin Dynasty
1279 to 1368	Yuan (Mongol) Dynasty 1275–1292 Visit of Marco Polo
1368 to 1644	Ming Dynasty

1644 to 1911	Qing (Manchu) Dynasty 1839–1842 Opium War with Great Britain; beginning of foreign concessions 1850–1864 Taiping Rebellion 1900 Boxer Rebellion—Chinese tried to expel foreigners (unsuccessfully)
1911 to 1949	Republic of China May 4, 1919 Massive protest against Versailles Treaty to end War World I which gave certain rights to Japan 1927 Split between Nationalists and Communists 1937 to 1945 War with Japan 1945 to 1949 Civil War—Nationalists and Communists
1949	People's Republic of China established
1966 to 1976	Cultural Revolution 1971 PRC admitted to United Nations 1972 President Nixon visits China

BIBLIOGRAPHY

BOOKS

Butterfield, Fox. *China: Alive in the Bitter Sea.* New York: Times Books, 1982.

Chapman, H. Owen. *The Chinese Revolution, 1926–1927.* London: Constable and Co., 1928.

Ch'en, Jerome. *Yuan Shih-Kai.* Berkeley: Stanford University Press, 1972.

Chesneaux, Jean, Françoise Le Barbier, and Marie-Claire Bergère. *China from the 1911 Revolution to Liberation.* New York: Random House, 1977.

Clubb, O. Edmund. *Communism in China as Reported from Hankow in 1932.* New York: Columbia University Press, 1968.

Collis, Maurice. *Foreign Mud.* London: Faber and Faber, 1964.

Coye, Molly C., Jon Livingston, and Jean Highland, eds. *China Yesterday and Today.* New York: Bantam, 1984.

Dingle, Edwin J. *China's Revolution: 1911–1912.* Shanghai: 1912.

Dollar, Robert. *The Private Diary of Robert Dollar.* San Francisco: W. S. Van Cott and Co., 1912.

Eberhard, Wolfram. *The Local Cultures of South and East China.* Leiden: E. J. Brill, 1968.

Elvin, Mark, and G. William Skinner, eds. *The Chinese City Between Two Worlds.* Berkeley: Stanford University Press, 1974.

Fairbanks, John King. *The Cambridge History of China,* Vol. XII, Part 1. New York: Cambridge University Press, 1983.

Fairbanks, John King. *Chinabound.* New York: Harper & Row, 1982.

Franz, Michael. *The Taiping Rebellion,* Vol. I. Seattle: University of Washington Press, 1966.

Frillman, Paul, and Graham Peck. *China: The Remembered Life.* Boston: Houghton Mifflin, 1968.

Gasster, Michael. *China's Struggle to Modernize.* New York: Knopf, 1972.

Gasster, Michael. *Chinese Intellectuals of the Revolution of 1911.* Seattle: University of Washington Press, 1969.

Groussett, René. *The Rise and Splendor of the Chinese Empire.* Berkeley: University of California Press, 1953.

Hsueh, Chun-tu. *Huang Hsing and the Chinese Revolution.* Berkeley: Stanford University Press, 1961.

Huang, Ray. *1587. A Year of No Significance. The Ming Dynasty in Decline.* New Haven: Yale University Press, 1981.

Hucker, Charles O. *China's Imperial Past.* Berkeley: Stanford University Press, 1975.

Karnow, Stanley. *Mao and China: From Revolution to Revolution.* New York: Viking, 1972.

Kates, George N. *The Years That Were Fat: The Last of Old China.* Cambridge, Mass.: M.I.T. Press, 1952.

Kramer, Paul, ed. *The Last Manchu: The Autobiography of Pu Yi, Last Emperor of China.* New York: G. P. Putnam's Sons, 1967.

Lo, Ruth Earnshaw, and Katherine S. Kinderman. *In the Eye of the Typhoon: An American Woman Shares in the Upheavals of China's Cultural Revolution, 1966–1978.* New York: Harcourt, 1980.

Matthews, Jay and Linda. *One Billion: A China Chronicle.* New York: Random House, 1983

Meskill, John. *The Pattern of Chinese History.* Boston: Heath, 1965.

North, Robert C. *Chinese Communism.* New York: McGraw-Hill, 1970.

Schneider, Laurence A. *A Madman of Ch'u.* Berkeley: University of California Press, 1980.

Schwarcz, Vera. *Long Road Home.* New Haven: Yale University Press, 1984.

Sheehan, Vincent. *Personal History*. Garden City: Garden City Publishing Co., 1937.

Sheridan, James. *Chinese Warlord: The Career of Feng Yu-hsiang*. Berkeley: Stanford University Press, 1966.

Spence, Jonathan. *Emperor of China*. New York: Knopf, 1974.

Spence, Jonathan. *The Gate of Heavenly Peace: The Chinese and Their Revolution, 1895–1980*. New York: Viking, 1981.

Spence, Jonathan. *To Change China*. Boston: Little, Brown, 1969.

Strong, Anna Louise. *China's Millions: The Revolutionary Struggles from 1927 to 1935*. New York: Knight Publishing Co., 1935.

Terrill, Ross. *Flowers on an Iron Tree: Five Cities of China*. Boston: Little, Brown, 1975.

Terrill, Ross. *The White-Boned Demon: A Biography of Madame Mao Zedong*. New York: Morrow, 1984.

Warner, Marina. *The Dragon Empress*. New York: Macmillan, 1972.

Wilson, Dick. *The Long March*. New York: Viking, 1971.

Witke, Roxanne. *Comrade Chiang Ching*. Boston: Little, Brown, 1977.

DISSERTATION

Rowe, William Townsend. "Urban Society in Late Imperial China; Hankow 1796–1889." Columbia University, 1980.

PERIODICALS

China News Analysis. No. 655 (April 14, 1967); No. 656 (April 21, 1967); No. 661 (May 26, 1967); No. 667 (July 7, 1967); No. 671 (August 4, 1967); No. 676 (September 8, 1967); No. 680 (October 6, 1967).

Oxenham, E. L. "History of Han Yang and Hankow." *China Review*, No. 6 (June 1873), pp. 366–370.

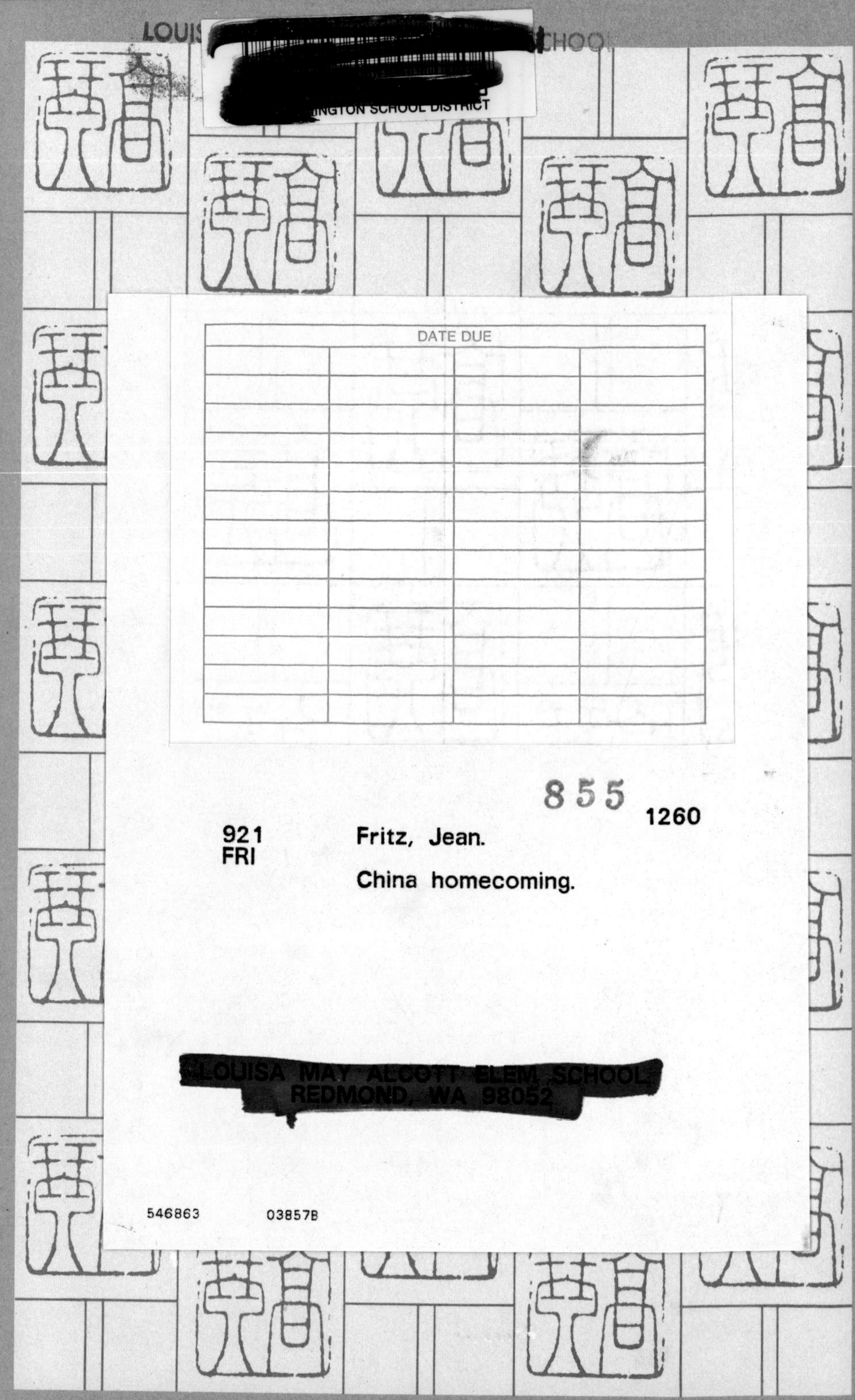